Advanced Metasearch Engine Technology

Advanced Metasearch Engine Technology

Weiyi Meng and Clement T. Yu

ISBN: 978-3-031-00715-6 paperback
ISBN: 978-3-031-01843-5 ebook

DOI 10.1007/978-3-031-01843-5

A Publication in the Springer series
SYNTHESIS LECTURES ON DATA MANAGEMENT

Lecture #11
Series Editor: M. Tamer Özsu, *University of Waterloo*
Series ISSN
Synthesis Lectures on Data Management
Print 2153-5418 Electronic 2153-5426

Synthesis Lectures on Data Management

Editor
M. Tamer Özsu, *University of Waterloo*

Synthesis Lectures on Data Management is edited by Tamer Özsu of the University of Waterloo. The series will publish 50- to 125 page publications on topics pertaining to data management. The scope will largely follow the purview of premier information and computer science conferences, such as ACM SIGMOD, VLDB, ICDE, PODS, ICDT, and ACM KDD. Potential topics include, but not are limited to: query languages, database system architectures, transaction management, data warehousing, XML and databases, data stream systems, wide scale data distribution, multimedia data management, data mining, and related subjects.

Advanced Metasearch Engine Technology
Weiyi Meng and Clement T. Yu
2010

Web Page Recommendation Models: Theory and Algorithms
Sule Gündüz-Ögüdücü
2010

Multidimensional Databases and Data Warehousing
Christian S. Jensen, Torben Bach Pedersen, and Christian Thomsen
2010

Database Replication
Bettina Kemme, Ricardo Jimenez Peris, and Marta Patino-Martinez
2010

Relational and XML Data Exchange
Marcelo Arenas, Pablo Barcelo, Leonid Libkin, and Filip Murlak
2010

User-Centered Data Management
Tiziana Catarci, Alan Dix, Stephen Kimani, and Giuseppe Santucci
2010

Advanced Metasearch Engine Technology

Weiyi Meng
SUNY Binghamtom

Clement T. Yu
University of Illinois at Chicago

SYNTHESIS LECTURES ON DATA MANAGEMENT #11

ABSTRACT

Among the search tools currently on the Web, search engines are the most well known thanks to the popularity of major search engines such as Google and Yahoo!. While extremely successful, these major search engines do have serious limitations.

This book introduces large-scale metasearch engine technology, which has the potential to overcome the limitations of the major search engines. Essentially, a metasearch engine is a search system that supports unified access to multiple existing search engines by passing the queries it receives to its component search engines and aggregating the returned results into a single ranked list. A large-scale metasearch engine has thousands or more component search engines. While metasearch engines were initially motivated by their ability to combine the search coverage of multiple search engines, there are also other benefits such as the potential to obtain better and fresher results and to reach the Deep Web.

The following major components of large-scale metasearch engines will be discussed in detail in this book: search engine selection, search engine incorporation, and result merging. Highly scalable and automated solutions for these components are emphasized. The authors make a strong case for the viability of the large-scale metasearch engine technology as a competitive technology for Web search.

KEYWORDS

metasearch engine, large-scale metasearch engine, search broker, distributed information retrieval, federated search system, search engine selection, database selection, search result extraction, wrapper generation, result merging, collection fusion

Contents

Preface

The World Wide Web has become the largest information source in recent years and developing advanced search tools has been a key research and development activity of the Internet technology. Among the search tools currently on the Web, search engines are the most well known thanks to the popularity of major search engines such as Google and Yahoo!. While extremely successful, these major search engines do have serious limitations. For example, each of them only covers a small fraction of the full contents available on the Web, and their crawling based technology has difficulty in fully reaching the so-called *deep Web*, although much progress on this aspect has been made recently, and in keeping up with the changes and expansion of the Web content.

In this book, we introduce the metasearch engine technology, which has the potential to overcome the limitations of the major search engines. A metasearch engine is a search system that supports unified access to some existing search engines. Essentially, a metasearch engine passes the queries it receives to other search engines, and when the results are returned from the invoked search engines, it aggregates the results into a single ranked list and presents them to the user. While metasearch engines were initially motivated by their ability to combine the search coverage of multiple search engines, there are additional benefits such as the potential to obtain better and fresher results and to reach the deep Web.

In this book, we emphasize the concept of *large-scale metasearch engine*. Such a metasearch engine is connected to thousands or more search engines. To build and maintain large-scale metasearch engines, *advanced metasearch search engine technology* with highly scalable and automated solutions for several key components is needed. This book aims to provide an in-depth and comprehensive coverage of advanced metasearch engine technology. We will make a strong case for the viability of the large-scale metasearch engines as a competitive technology for Web search. The following major components of large-scale metasearch engine will be discussed in detail in this book: search engine selection – a component that identifies search engines that are most likely to provide useful results for any give query; search engine incorporation – a component that interacts with various search engines, including passing queries from the metasearch engine to local search engines and extracting the search results from response pages returned from different search engines; and result merging – a component that merges results returned from different search engines into a single ranked list. Advanced metasearch engine technology includes highly accurate and scalable search engine selection algorithms, highly automated search engine incorporation techniques, and highly effective result merging methods.

This book can be used as part of Web technology related courses such as Web data management and information retrieval. It can also be a reference book for IT professionals, especially researchers and developers in the Web search area.

Weiyi Meng and Clement T. Yu
November 2010

Acknowledgments

We like to express our deep gratitude to the series editor of the Synthesis Lectures on Data Management, Dr. M. Tamer Özsu, who read the entire manuscript carefully and provided very valuable and constructive suggestions, which have helped improve the book significantly. We also like to thank Hongkun Zhao and Can Lin for reading parts of the manuscript and providing valuable comments. We are also grateful to the editor of the book, Diane Cerra, for her help in the course of preparing the book.

Weiyi Meng and Clement T. Yu
November 2010

CHAPTER 1

Introduction

The World Wide Web (simply referred to as the Web) has emerged as the largest information source in recent years. People all over the world use the Web to find needed information on a regular basis. Indeed, the Web has already become an important part in many people's daily lives.

The Web has been expanding very rapidly since its emergence in 1990. It can be divided into the *surface Web* and the *deep Web* (or *hidden Web*). The former refers to the collection of Web pages that are publicly and directly accessible without the need to go through a registration, login, or the interface of a search engine. Usually, each such page has a static logical address called Uniform Resource Locator or URL. Web pages in the surface Web are usually hyperlinked and can be accessed by ordinary Web crawlers[1] via hyperlinks. The exact size of the surface Web is unknown but the size of the indexed Web, which is a subset of the surface Web, was estimated to be as much as 55 billion Web pages in August 2010 according to `http://www.worldwidewebsize.com/`. The deep Web contains Web pages that cannot be crawled by ordinary Web crawlers. They include Web contents that are not publicly accessible or are dynamically generated. As an example, consider the case where a publisher has accumulated many articles in digital format, but these articles are not placed on the surface Web (i.e., there are no static URLs for them), and they are only accessible by Web users through the publisher's search engine, then these articles belong to the deep Web. Web pages that are dynamically generated using data stored in database systems also belong to the deep Web. The deep Web contained approximately 1 trillion pages of information by the end of 2009 (Zillman, P., 2009). Both the surface Web and the deep Web are expanding rapidly.

How to help ordinary users find desired information from the Web has been one of the central issues in the Web technology area since early 1990s. Over these years, many search engines have been created by researchers and developers, and they have become the most popular tools for people to find desired information on the Web. Search engines are generally easy-to-use tools with a simple query interface. A user types in his/her query – usually a few words that reflect the user's information needs – to the query interface of a search engine, and the search engine finds the best matches from its repository. Based on what type of data is searched, there are document-driven search engines and database-driven search engines. The former searches documents (Web pages) while the latter searches data items from database systems through Web-based search interfaces. Database-driven search engines are mostly employed for e-commerce applications such as buying cars or books. This book focuses on searching text documents only.

[1]Web crawler will be discussed in Section 1.3.2.

Due to the huge size and the fast expansion of the Web, each search engine can only cover a small portion of the Web. One of the largest search engines on the Web, Google (`http://www.google.com/`), for example, can search as many as 35 billion pages (`http://www.worldwidewebsize.com/`), which is still a small fraction of the entire Web. It is widely observed that different search engines cover different, albeit overlapping, portions of the Web. One effective way to increase the search coverage of the Web is to combine the coverage of multiple search engines. Systems that perform such combination are called *metasearch engines*. A metasearch engine can be considered as a system that supports unified access to multiple existing search engines. In a typical session, using a metasearch engine, the user submits a query to the metasearch engine, which passes the query to its component search engines; when the metasearch engine receives the search results returned from its component search engines, it merges these results into a single ranked list and displays them to the user.

Although the focus of the book is on advanced metasearch engine technology, it is still important that the readers have a good grasp on how a typical search engine works. The technology behind search engines has its root in a computer science discipline known as *information retrieval* or *text retrieval*. In this chapter, we will first provide a brief discussion on different ways to find information on the Web, and then review some basic concepts and algorithms in text retrieval and search engine technology. The last section of this chapter will provide an overview of the rest of the book.

1.1 FINDING INFORMATION ON THE WEB

There are two basic paradigms for finding information on the Web: *browsing* and *searching*. Most, if not all, Web users have used both methods to find the information they need from the Web. In this section, we discuss these two paradigms in more detail.

1.1.1 BROWSING

Browsing consists of two steps: finding a starting page and following the links in the current page. If a user already knows the URL of the starting page, the user can type in the URL of the page directly in the address bar of the Web browser. Many users save the URLs of the pages they frequently visit in the bookmarks or favorites list of their browsers. In this case, a user can also launch the starting page from the bookmarked list. The number of URLs that a user can remember or save in the bookmark list is very limited. Another widely used technique to find a starting page is *searching*, where a search is conducted using a set of terms, and one of the result pages returned from a search engine is used as the starting page. Thus, searching and browsing are often used together by Web users in their pursuit to find desired information. After the starting page is determined, it becomes the current page and the user can click on any clickable text in the current page to display the page whose URL is encoded in the clickable text. The clickable text is also known as *anchor text* as the text is enclosed between the HTML anchor tags as in <a href="URL"> anchor text </a>. Anchor text may provide a clue on the contents of the page whose URL is the value of the "href" attribute of the anchor tag.

To facilitate browsing, the developers of Web portals, Web sites and Web pages have the responsibility to make browsing-based information finding as easy as possible. Yahoo! is probably the most popular Web portal, and it places millions of Web pages and Web sites into many categories and organizes these categories in a hierarchical structure. As a category hierarchy can narrow down the information scope from one level to the next level quickly, it reduces the information finding effort. Many Web sites also provide a *sitemap*, which shows the accessible pages in hierarchical fashion to make browsing easier. In specific Web pages, the anchor text for each link should be sufficiently informative about the contents of the linked page.

1.1.2 SEARCHING

Searching is the second most popular activity on the Internet behind only activities related to sending and receiving emails. Searching is composed of three steps: identify a search engine to use, compose a query, and go through the list of results to identify relevant ones. The third step is fairly straightforward as the results returned by most search engines contain adequate information for users to determine whether the full pages are worth further examination. In the following, we discuss how to determine the appropriate search engine to use and how to compose appropriate queries.

Determine Appropriate Search Engines

Most users are familiar with one or more major search engines on the Web. According to a comScore (`http://www.comscore.com/`) report released in August 2010 (comScore report, 2010), the following are the most popular search engines in the United States: Google (`http://www.google.com/`), Yahoo! (`http://www.yahoo.com/`), Bing (`http://www.bing.com/`), Ask (`http://www.ask.com/`), and AOL (`http://www.aol.com/`). They occupy 65.4%, 17.4%, 11.1%, 3.8% and 2.3% of the search market, respectively. However, there are actually millions of search engines on the Web and only a small number of them are general-purpose search engines that aim to provide complete search coverage of the Web. Most search engines are small with a confined search scope. For example, most organizations such as universities, newspapers and book publishers have their own search engines covering only Web contents they produce. As another example, there are also many domain-specific or vertical search engines that cover Web pages in a specific domain or subdomain such as medicine, news, movies, and sports. Furthermore, there are also search engines that cover contents in the deep Web. Small and domain-specific search engines can often return more relevant and more up-to-date results than the major search engines because their search domains are more focused and it is easier to keep smaller datasets fresh. Moreover, deep Web search engines can return results that are often not available from major search engines because major search engines search mostly the surface Web.

From the above analysis about search engines, we can see that identifying an appropriate search engine to use for a given information need is not an easy task. First, most users are not even aware of the vast majority of the available search engines. There is currently no complete directory of all search engines on the Web. The current most complete directory at CompletePlanet (`http://`

aip.completeplanet.com/) lists about 70,000 search engines, a small fraction of what is believed to be available. Second, there is no systematic quality evaluation of all the search engines on the Web. Therefore, it is hard for ordinary users to know which search engines are most appropriate for his or her information need. Because of these difficulties, most users just settle with using some of the popular search engines for their search needs. More experienced users can often find more appropriate search engines through personal experience and recommendation from others. Nevertheless, it is highly desirable to have a complete directory of all search engines accompanied with information about their quality as part of the Web infrastructure. It would even be better to have a search engine recommendation system that is as easy to use as a regular search engine.

Form Appropriate Search Queries

Document-driven search engines usually have a simple query interface – a textbox that allows users to enter their queries and a submit button. Analyses of user queries submitted to search engines have revealed that most users just submit simple and short queries – an indication that most users have little or no training about writing good queries. For example, an analysis of approximately 1 billion queries submitted to the AltaVista search engine (http://www.altavista.com/) in 1998 revealed the following interesting characteristics about Web search queries (Silverstein et al., 1999):

- Queries were usually short: The average number of terms in a query was 2.35, about 26% of the queries had a single term, and less than 13% of the queries had more than three terms.
- Most queries used no operators: About 80% of the queries did not use any operators.

Some of the operators that are widely supported by search engines include: Boolean AND – a Web page must contain all the query terms in order to satisfy the query; Boolean OR – a Web page is required to contain at least one of the query terms; and Boolean NOT – a Web page must not contain the query terms qualified by NOT. Some search engines also support certain form of proximity query that requires specified query terms to appear close to each other in a Web page for it to be qualified.

Users can improve the quality of their queries by following the suggestions below:

1. Avoid submitting ambiguous queries. A query is ambiguous if it has multiple very different interpretations. For example, the query "windows" may be interpreted as Microsoft Windows operating system or windows of a building. An effective way to avoid ambiguous queries is to avoid overly short queries. With longer queries, each term has more terms from the same query as context in helping determine the correct meaning of the term. There is evidence that users are increasingly submitting longer queries. By the end of 2007, queries submitted to Google had averaged 4 terms for the first time (Ussery, B., 2008).

2. Use the appropriate operators. If a user plans to use a search engine frequently, then it is worth making an effort to find out what operators are supported by the search engine. These operators often have different formats in different search engines. Furthermore, many search engines apply a default operator to user queries if no operator is specified. For example, Google uses Boolean AND as the default operator.

In another study, Broder, A. (2002) analyzed users' needs behind their queries based on a user survey and found that users often have different needs when submitting their queries to a search engine. Based on this study, Broder classified Web queries into the following three classes according to the search needs.

1. *Navigational queries*. This type of queries aims to find a particular Web page or Web site the user has in mind. For example, the purpose of query "Binghamton University" is to find the homepage of Binghamton University, i.e., `http://www.binghamton.edu/`. Any page other than this homepage won't be considered as correct. Usually, users who submit such queries are aware of the Web pages they seek, perhaps because they had visited the pages before.

2. *Informational queries*. This class of queries aims to find certain information from the Web, which may be spread over multiple pages. Users who submit this type of queries are usually satisfied as far as one of the pages that contain the desired information is retrieved.

3. *Transactional queries*. The purpose of this class of queries is to find a Web site to perform certain transactions interactively. Examples of transactions include shopping, downloading music and movies, and signing up for certain services.

According to the analysis of 1,000 queries, 48% are informational queries, 30% are transactional queries and 20% are navigational queries (Broder, A., 2002).

The purpose of analyzing user queries is to devise better query evaluation techniques.

1.2 A BRIEF OVERVIEW OF TEXT RETRIEVAL

Text (information) retrieval deals with the problem of finding relevant (useful) documents for any given query from a collection of text documents. Text retrieval technology has a profound and direct influence on Web search engines. In fact, the first generation search engines (around 1995-1997) were built almost entirely based on traditional text retrieval technology where web pages were treated as text documents. In this section, we provide a brief overview of some basic concepts in classical text retrieval. The overview is primarily based on the *vector space model* where both documents and user queries are represented as vectors of terms with weights (Salton and McGill, 1983). Readers who want to read more about this subject are referred to relevant textbooks such as (Salton and McGill, 1983), (Frakes and Baeza-Yates, 1992), (Manning et al., 2008), and (Croft et al., 2009).

1.2.1 SYSTEM ARCHITECTURE

The architecture of a basic text retrieval system is shown in Fig. 1.1. Documents in the document collection of a text retrieval system are preprocessed to identify terms representing each document, to collect certain statistics about the terms, and to organize the information in a certain format (i.e., the *index* in Fig. 1.1) that facilitate fast computation of the similarity of each document with respect to any query.

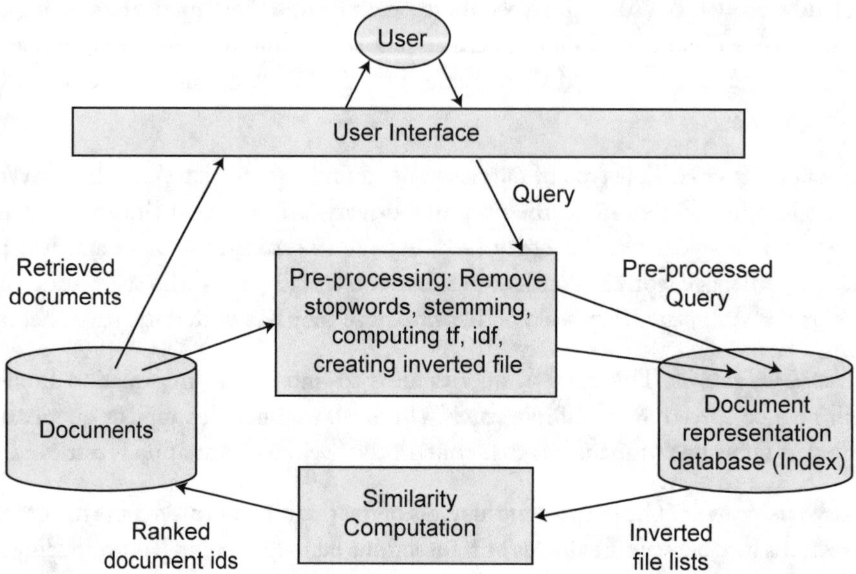

Figure 1.1: Architecture of a Basic Text Retrieval System.

When a user query is received, the text retrieval system processes the query by first identifying terms that represent the query and then computing the weights of the terms, which reflect the importance of terms in representing the content of the query. Then the system computes the similarities of the documents to the query using the pre-built index and ranks the documents in descending order of their similarities. More details about these concepts and operations will be provided in the next several subsections.

1.2.2 DOCUMENT REPRESENTATION

The contents of a document may be represented by the words contained in it. Some words such as "a," "of" and "is" do not contain topical content information. These words are called *stop words* and are often not used. Variations of the same word may be mapped to the same term. For example, the words "compute," "computing" and "computation" can be denoted by the term "comput." This can be achieved by a *stemming program*, which removes suffixes or replaces them by other characters. After removing stop words and stemming, each document can be logically represented by a vector of n terms (Baeza-Yates and Ribeiro-Neto, 1999), where n is the total number of distinct terms in the set of all documents in a document collection. It should be noted that different text retrieval systems often employ different stop word lists and/or stemming algorithms. Many current search engines do not actually remove stop words. Furthermore, a term does not necessarily mean a single word; it could be a phrase.

Suppose document d is represented by the vector $(d_1, \ldots, d_i, \ldots, d_n)$, where d_i is a number (called *weight*) indicating the importance of the i-th term in representing the contents of the document. If a term does not appear in d, its weight will be zero. When a term is present in d, its weight is usually computed based on two factors, namely the *term frequency* (*tf*) factor and the *document frequency* (*df*) factor. The *tf* of a term in a document is the number of times the term appears in the document. Intuitively, the higher the *tf* of a term is, the more important the term is. As a result, the *term frequency weight* (*tfw*) of a term in a document is usually a monotonically increasing function of its *tf*. The *df* of a term is the number of documents containing the term in the entire document collection. Usually, the higher the *df* of a term is, the less important the term is in differentiating different documents. Thus, the weight of a term with respect to *df* is usually a monotonically decreasing function of its *df* and is called the *inverse document frequency weight* (*idfw*). The weight of a term in a document can be the product of its term frequency weight and its inverse document frequency weight, i.e., *tfw* * *idfw*. The weight of a term in a document may also be affected by other factors such as where it appears in the document; for example, the weight may be increased if the term appears in the title of the document.

A typical query for text retrieval is also written in text. As such, it can be treated like a document and transformed into an n-dimensional vector as well using the method described above.

1.2.3 DOCUMENT-QUERY MATCHING

After all documents and a query have been represented as vectors of the same dimension, a similarity between the query vector and each document vector can be calculated using a *similarity function*. Then documents whose corresponding vectors have high similarities with the query vector are retrieved. Let $q = (q_1, \ldots, q_n)$ and $d = (d_1, \ldots, d_n)$ be the vectors of a query and a document, respectively.

A simple similarity function is the following dot (inner) product function:

$$\mathrm{dot}(q, d) = \sum_{i=1}^{n} q_i * d_i. \tag{1.1}$$

This function gives higher similarities to documents that have more important terms in common with the query. One problem with this simple similarity function is that it is biased in favor of longer documents because they are more likely to contain the terms in the query. One popular way to overcome the problem associated with the dot product function is to divide the dot product by the product of the lengths of the two vectors, namely the document vector and the query vector. The new similarity function is known as the *Cosine function* (Salton and McGill, 1983):

$$\cos(q, d) = \frac{\sum_{i=1}^{n} q_i * d_i}{\sqrt{\sum_{i=1}^{n} q_i^2} * \sqrt{\sum_{i=1}^{n} d_i^2}}. \tag{1.2}$$

The *Cosine function* of two vectors has a geometric interpretation – it is the cosine of the angle between the two vectors. In other words, the *Cosine function* measures the angular distance between a query vector and a document vector. When the vectors have non-negative weights, the *Cosine function* always returns a value within [0, 1]. Its value is 0 when the query and the document do not share terms (i.e., when the angle between the two vectors is 90°); its value is 1 when the query and the document vectors are identical or one vector is a positive constant multiple of the other (i.e., when the angle is 0°).

There are other similarity functions, and some of them also consider the proximity of the query terms in a document. The closer the query terms appear in a document, the more likely the document will retain the meaning of the query, and thus the similarity between the query and the document should be higher. To support proximity based match, for any given document and a term, the positions of the term in the document need to be collected and stored as part of the search index.

There are also several other text retrieval models. In the basic *Boolean retrieval model*, documents are retrieved based on whether they contain the query terms, and the weights of the terms are not considered. A Boolean query can contain one or more Boolean operators (AND, OR and NOT). In the *probabilistic model* (Robertson and Sparck Jones, 1976; Yu and Salton, 1976), the documents are ranked in descending order of the probability that a document will be *relevant* to a query. The probabilities are estimated based on the distribution of the query terms in relevant and irrelevant documents. One of the most widely used similarity functions based on the probabilistic model is the *Okapi function* (Robertson and Walker, 1999). In recent years, *language model* has also been applied to information retrieval with good success (Ponte and Croft, 1998; Zhai and Lafferty, 2004). In this approach, for a given query, we estimate the probability that the query can be generated based on each document and then rank the documents in descending order of the probabilities. Some other language models also exist (Croft et al., 2009).

1.2.4 QUERY EVALUATION

Computing the similarity between a query and every document directly is inefficient because most documents do not have any term in common with a given query, and computing the similarities for these documents is a waste of resources. To improve the efficiency, an *inverted file index* is created in advance. For each term t_i, an inverted list of the format $I(t_i) = [(D_{i_1}, w_{i_1 i}), \ldots, (D_{i_k}, w_{i_k i})]$ with a header is generated and stored, where D_{i_j} is the identifier of a document containing t_i, $w_{i_j i}$ is the weight of t_i in D_{i_j}, $1 \le j \le k$, and k is the number of documents containing t_i. In addition, a hash table, which is a table-like data structure, is used to map each query term to the header of the inverted list of the term. The inverted file and the hash table enable efficient computation of the similarities of all the documents that have non-zero similarities with any query. Specifically, consider a query with m terms. For each query term, the hash table is used to locate the term's inverted list. The m inverted lists contain essentially all the information needed to compute the similarities between the query and all the documents containing at least one query term.

A widely used query evaluation strategy is the *document-at-a-time strategy* (Turtle and Flood, 1995), which computes the similarity for one document at a time and only documents that contain at least one query term are considered. The basic idea of this strategy is as follows. In many text retrieval systems, the inverted file is too large to be kept in main memory and is thus stored on disk. If the inverted file is on disk, then at the beginning of evaluating a query, the inverted lists of all the query terms are first brought into main memory. Then the similarities of the documents, each containing at least one query term, are computed, one document at a time. Suppose a query has m terms. Each term corresponds to an inverted list in which documents containing the term have their identifiers in ascending order. The similarity is computed by performing an m-way merge of these inverted lists as illustrated in the following Example 1.1. Due to the synchronized scan of the m inverted lists, one scan of each of the inverted lists of query terms is sufficient for the evaluation of the query.

Example 1.1 Fig. 1.2 shows the document-term matrix for an example document collection with five documents and five distinct terms. For simplicity, the weights are raw term frequencies, and the dot product function is used as the similarity function here.

	t_1	t_2	t_3	t_4	t_5
D_1	2	1	1	0	0
D_2	0	2	1	1	0
D_3	1	0	1	1	0
D_4	2	1	2	2	0
D_5	0	2	0	1	2

Figure 1.2: Document-Term Matrix.

From the matrix in Fig. 1.2, we can obtain following inverted file lists:

$$
\begin{aligned}
I(t_1) &= [(D_1, 2), (D_3, 1), (D_4, 2)], \\
I(t_2) &= [(D_1, 1), (D_2, 2), (D_4, 1), (D_5, 2)], \\
I(t_3) &= [(D_1, 1), (D_2, 1), (D_3, 1), (D_4, 2)], \\
I(t_4) &= [(D_2, 1), (D_3, 1), (D_4, 2), (D_5, 1)], \\
I(t_5) &= [(D_5, 2)].
\end{aligned}
$$

Let q be a query with two terms t_1 and t_3 with their weights both being 1 (i.e., they each appears exactly once).

We now apply the document-at-a-time strategy to calculate the similarities of documents with respect to q. We first fetch the inverted file lists for the two query terms into main memory. After $I(t_1) = [(D_1, 2), (D_3, 1), (D_4, 2)]$ and $I(t_3) = [(D_1, 1), (D_2, 1), (D_3, 1), (D_4, 2)]$ are fetched, each document appearing in the lists is considered in a synchronized manner. The first document in both lists is D_1 (i.e., D_1 contains both query terms t_1 and t_3), and its similarity with the query can be computed from the weights 2 (for t_1) and 1 (for t_3) and the query, using the dot product function, i.e., $\text{dot}(q, D_1) = 1 * 2 + 1 * 1 = 3$. The next items in the two lists are $(D_3, 1)$ and $(D_2, 1)$. Since $D_2 < D_3$ (in terms of document identifiers), D_2 is considered first. It can be determined that D_2 does not contain t_1. Therefore, the similarity of D_2 can be computed based on $(D_2, 1)$ alone, $\text{dot}(q, D_2) = 1 * 1 = 1$. Once $(D_2, 1)$ is processed, the next item in $I(t_3)$, namely $(D_3, 1)$, is considered, leading to the computation of the similarity of D_3, using information from both $I(t_1)$ and $I(t_3)$, i.e., $\text{dot}(q, D_3) = 1 * 1 + 1 * 1 = 2$. Similarly, the similarity of D_4 can be computed as $\text{dot}(q, D_4) = 1 * 2 + 1 * 2 = 4$. Since $(D_4, 2)$ is the last item in both lists, the similarity computation process ends.

Another well-known query evaluation strategy is the *term-at-a-time strategy* (Turtle and Flood, 1995). This strategy processes the inverted lists of the query terms one by one; after the inverted list of a query term is processed, the contribution of this term to the overall similarity between the query and each document that contains this query term is computed and then added to the contribution by the query terms that have already been processed. When the inverted lists for all query terms are processed, the final similarity between the query and each document containing at least one query term is computed.

Example 1.2 We illustrate the term-at-a-time strategy using the documents and query from Example 1.1. Suppose query term t_1 is considered first. We first obtain $I(t_1)$. Since $I(t_1)$ contains D_1, D_3 and D_4, the following intermediate similarities are obtained after t_1 is processed: $\text{dot}(q, D_1) = 1 * 2 = 2$, $\text{dot}(q, D_3) = 1 * 1 = 1$, $\text{dot}(q, D_4) = 1 * 2 = 2$. For query term t_3, we obtain $I(t_3)$. By adding the contribution of t_3 to the partial similarities that have been obtained earlier, we obtain the following final similarities: $\text{dot}(q, D_1) = 2 + 1 * 1 = 3$, $\text{dot}(q, D_2) = 0 + 1 * 1 = 1$, $\text{dot}(q, D_3) = 1 + 1 * 1 = 2$, and $\text{dot}(q, D_4) = 2 + 1 * 2 = 4$.

There are a number of pruning strategies to reduce the computational overhead of the above two basic evaluation strategies (Turtle and Flood, 1995).

1.2.5 RETRIEVAL EFFECTIVENESS MEASURES

The goal of text retrieval is to find documents that are *relevant* (useful) to the person who submits a query and rank these documents high in the result list. The retrieval effectiveness of a text retrieval system is often measured by a pair of quantities known as *recall* and *precision*. Suppose, for a given user query, the set of relevant documents in the document collection is known. Then recall is the proportion of the relevant documents that are retrieved and precision is the proportion of the retrieved documents that are relevant. As an example, suppose there are 10 relevant documents for a query and among the 20 retrieved documents, 6 are relevant. Then for this query, the recall is $6/10 = 0.6$ and the precision is $6/20 = 0.3$.

To evaluate the effectiveness of a text retrieval system, a set of test queries is often used. For each query, the set of relevant documents is identified in advance. For each test query, a precision value for each distinct recall value is obtained. Usually, only eleven recall values, 0.0, 0.1, ..., 1.0, are considered. When the precision values at each recall value are averaged over all test queries, an average recall-precision curve is obtained.

There are also many other retrieval effectiveness measures for text retrieval systems. In the context of search engines, it is often impossible to know the complete set of relevant documents for test queries. In such cases, some precision-oriented measures can be used based on certain top ranked results. For example, *precision at n* can be used to compute the precision of the top n ranked results for some n. Readers may refer to the book by Voorhees and Harman (2005) for more information regarding the evaluation methodologies and the evaluation measures.

1.3 A BRIEF OVERVIEW OF SEARCH ENGINE TECHNOLOGY

The earliest Web search engines were basically text retrieval systems for Web pages. However, the Web environment has some special characteristics that make building modern search engines significantly different from building traditional text retrieval systems. In this section, we provide a brief overview of these special characteristics as well as search engine building techniques that address/explore these characteristics.

1.3.1 SPECIAL CHARACTERISTICS OF THE WEB

The following are some of the key special characteristics of the Web environment that have significant impact on search engine development.

1. Web pages are stored on a large number of autonomous Web servers. A method is needed to find them and fetch them so that they can be processed for later search.

2. Most Web pages are in HTML (HyperText Markup Language) format and the HTML tags often convey rich information regarding the terms in these pages. For example, a term appearing in the title of a page or a term that is highlighted by special font can provide a hint that the term is important in representing the contents of the page.

3. Web pages are linked to each other. A link from page P1 to page P2 allows a Web user to navigate from page P1 to page P2. Such a link also contains several pieces of information that are useful to improve retrieval effectiveness. First, the link indicates a good likelihood that the contents of the two pages are related [Davison, 2000]. Second, the author of page P1 considers page P2 to be valuable. Third, the clickable text associated with the link, called *anchor text* of the link, usually provides a short description of the linked page [Davison, 2000].

In this section we also discuss an issue that is important to both search engines and traditional text retrieval systems, but it has a special flavor in search engines. It is about the organization of search results on response pages.

1.3.2 WEB CRAWLER

A *Web crawler* is a program for fetching Web pages from remote Web servers. It is also known as *Web spider* and *Web robot*. They are widely used to build the Web page collection for a search engine.

The basic idea behind the crawler program is quite simple. Each Web page has a URL (Universal Resource Locator) that identifies the location of the page on the Web. A typical crawler takes one or more seed URLs as input to form an initial URL list. The crawler then repeats the following two steps until either no new URLs can be found or enough pages have been fetched: (1) Take the next URL from the URL list, establish connection to the server where the Web page resides, and fetch the corresponding Web page from its server by issuing an HTTP (HyperText Transfer Protocol) request to the server; (2) Extract new URLs from each fetched Web page and add them to the list. A crawler may fetch Web pages either breadth-first or depth-first. With breadth-first crawling, the URL list is implemented as a *queue* – new URLs are always added at the end of the list. With depth-first crawling, the URL list is implemented as a *stack* – the new URLs are always added at the beginning of the list.

By adding only new URLs of the Web pages that are related to a certain topic (say sports) to the URL list, the Web crawler becomes a *focused crawler* for the topic. Focused crawlers are useful for creating domain-specific or vertical search engines [Chakrabarti et al., 1999]. For a focused crawler to be effective, the crawler needs to accurately predict whether a URL will bring a page or pages related to the topic of interest. One technique useful for such prediction is to check whether the URL, the anchor text associated with the URL and the text adjacent to the anchor text, contain terms related to the topic.

One aspect in implementing a Web crawler is the ability to identify all (new) URLs from a Web page. This requires the identification of all possible HTML tags and tag attributes that may hold URLs. While most URLs appear in the anchor tag (e.g., <a href="URL" ...> ...</a>), URLs may also appear in other tags such as option tags as in < option value="URL" ...> ...</option >, area tags (map) as in < area href="URL" ...> ...</area >, and frame tags as in < frame src="URL" ...> ...</frame >. Frequently, a URL appearing in a Web page *P* does not contain the full path needed to locate the corresponding Web page from a Web browser. Instead, a partial or relative path is often used. In this case, a full path needs to be constructed by the crawler using the relative path and a base path associated with *P*.

When designing a Web crawler, it is important to be considerate to remote servers from which Web pages are fetched. *Rapid fires* (fetching a large number of Web pages from the same server in a short period of time) may overwhelm a server, effectively causing a denial-of-service attack to the server. A well-designed Web crawler should control the pace of fetching multiple pages from the same server by alternating fetches across a large number of different servers. Considerate Web crawlers should also follow the *Robot Exclusion Protocol* by not crawling the portion of a Web site that the Web server administrator does not want to be crawled. A Web server administrator can specify directories that can or cannot be crawled in a file named *robots.txt* on the Web server.

To speed up crawling or deal with large-scale crawling, a Web crawler may employ parallel crawling and/or distributed crawling. Parallel crawling can be achieved by using multiple threads or multiple computers to perform crawling from different servers simultaneously. Distributed crawling uses multiple computers at different geographical locations such that each computer can concentrate on fetching Web pages from Web servers that are closer to the computer, making crawling more efficient with reduced network delay.

1.3.3 UTILIZING TAG INFORMATION

Most Web pages are HTML pages and the HTML language contains a set of tags such as *title* and *font*. Most tags appear in pairs with one indicating the start and the other indicating the end. For example, in HTML, the starting and ending tags for title are < title > and </title >, respectively. In the context of search engine applications, tag information is primarily used to help determine the importance of index terms in representing the contents of a Web page.

In Section 1.2.2, we introduced a method that uses the term frequency and document frequency information of a term to compute the weight of the term in a document. We can also use tag information to influence the weight of a term. For example, Web page authors frequently use emphatic fonts such as **boldface**, *italics* and *underscore* as well as colors to highlight certain terms in a Web page. These terms can be considered as more important terms and therefore should be given higher weights. Conversely, terms in smaller fonts should be given lower weights. Other tags such as *title* and different levels of *header* can also be used to influence term weights. Many well-known search engines, including Google, have been known to assign higher weights to terms in titles.

A general approach to utilize tags to adjust term weights is as follows (Cutler et al., 1999). First, the set of all HTML tags is partitioned into a number of subsets. For example, the title tag could be a subset by itself, all list tags (namely "ul," "ol" and "dl") could be grouped together, and all emphatic tags could form a subset. Next, term occurrences in a page are partitioned into a number of classes, one class for each subset of tags. For example, all term occurrences appearing in the title form a class. Additionally, two other classes can also be formed for each page P. The first contains term occurrences in plain text (i.e., with no tags) and the second contains term occurrences that appear in the anchor texts associated with the back links of page P. Let n be the number of classes formed. With these classes, the term frequency of each term in a page can be represented as a *term frequency vector*: $tfv = (tf_1, \ldots, tf_n)$, where tf_i is the number of times the term appears in the i-th class, $i = 1, \ldots, n$. Finally, different degrees of importance can be assigned to different classes. Let $civ = (civ_1, \ldots, civ_n)$ be the *class importance vector* such that civ_i is the degree of importance of the i-th class, $i = 1, \ldots, n$. Based on vectors tfv and civ, the traditional term frequency weight formula can be extended into $\sum_{i=1}^{n} tf_i * civ_i$. This formula takes the frequencies of a term in different classes as well as the importance of each class into consideration. An interesting issue is how to find the optimal class importance vector that can yield the highest retrieval effectiveness. One method is to find an optimal or near optimal *civ* empirically based on a test dataset (Cutler et al., 1999).

1.3.4 UTILIZING LINK INFORMATION

The fact that there are extensive links between Web pages is probably one of the most significant differences between the documents in traditional text retrieval systems and those in search engines. The issue of how to utilize the link information to improve retrieval effectiveness has received a lot of attention by search engine researchers and developers. The best known approaches are based on exploring the observation that a link from page P_1 to page P_2 represents an endorsement of P_2 by the author of P_1. Of these methods, the most well known is the PageRank method developed by the founders of Google (Page et al., 1998). This method tries to find the overall importance of each Web page regardless of the contents of the page. In this section, we describe the basic ideas of this method.

The PageRank method views the Web as a gigantic directed graph $G(V, E)$, where V is the set of pages (vertices) and E is the set of links (directed edges). Each page may have a number of outgoing edges (forward links) and a number of incoming edges (back links). As observed above, when an author places a link in page P_1 to point to page P_2, the author considers page P_2 to be valuable. In other words, such a link can be viewed as a vote of support for page P_2. A page may have many back links, which can be aggregated in some way to reflect the overall importance of the page. The PageRank of a page is a measure of the relative importance of the page on the Web, and this measure is computed based on the link information (Page et al., 1998). The definition and computation of the PageRanks of Web pages are based on the following three main ideas.

1. Pages that have more back links are likely to be more important. Intuitively, a page with more back links receives the vote of support from more Web page authors. In other words, the importance of a page should be reflected by the popularity of the page among all Web page authors.

2. Pages that have more important pages pointing to it should have increased importance. In other words, not only the number but also the *significance* of the back links should be taken into consideration. Intuitively, important pages are likely to be published by important authors or organizations, and the endorsement of these authors/organizations should have more weight in determining the importance of a page. This has two implications. First, the importance of a page should be propagated to the pages it points to. Second, the computation of PageRanks is an iterative process because while a page's importance is affected by the pages that are linked to it, the importance of these pages themselves will be affected by other pages that have links pointing to them, and so on.

3. Pages that have more focused attention from the pages that point to them should receive more propagated importance from these pages. Intuitively, when a page has more forward links, it has less influence over the importance of each of the linked pages. Therefore, if a page has

more child pages, then it can only propagate a smaller fraction of its importance to each child page.

From the above discussion, it can be seen that it is natural to compute the PageRank of Web pages in a recursive manner. The PageRank of a page u is defined more formally as follows. Let F_u denote the set of pages u links to and B_u denote the set of pages that point to u (see Fig. 1.3). For a set X, let $|X|$ denote the number of items in X. The PageRank of u, denoted $R(u)$, is defined by the formula below:

$$R(u) = \sum_{v \in B_u} \frac{R(v)}{|F_v|}. \tag{1.3}$$

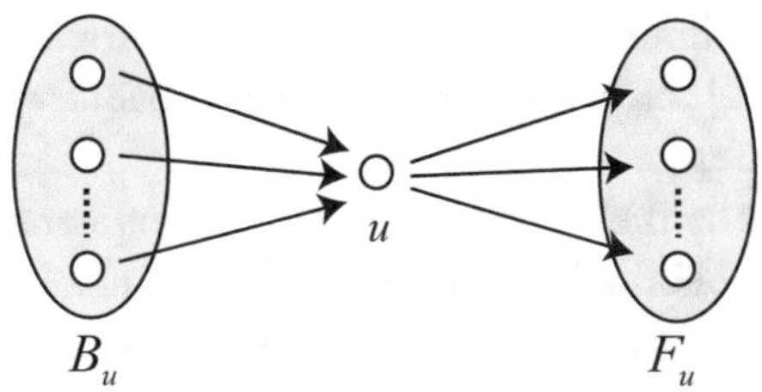

Figure 1.3: Page u and its Adjacent Pages.

It is not difficult to see that Formula (1.3) incorporates the three ideas we discussed earlier. First, the summation reflects the first idea, that is, more back links can lead to a larger PageRank. Second, having $R(v)$ in the numerator indicates that the PageRank of u becomes larger if page v is more important (i.e., has larger $R(v)$). Third, using $|F_v|$ in the denominator implies that the importance of a page is evenly divided and propagated to each of the pages it points to. Also notice that Formula (1.3) is recursive.

The PageRanks of the Web pages in a Web page graph can be computed as follows. First, an initial PageRank is assigned to all pages. Let N be the number of Web pages in the graph. Then use $1/N$ as the initial PageRank of each page. Next, Formula (1.3) is applied to compute the PageRanks in a number of iterations. In each iteration, the PageRank of a page is computed using the PageRanks of the pages that point to the page computed the previous iteration. Repeat this process until the PageRanks of all pages converge within a given threshold. Let $R_i(u)$ denote the rank of page u after the i-th iteration and $R(u)$ denote the initial rank assigned to page u. Then Formula (1.3) can be re-written as follows:

$$R_i(u) = \sum_{v \in B_u} \frac{R_{i-1}(v)}{|F_v|}. \tag{1.4}$$

Formula (1.4) can be expressed in matrix format as follows. Let M be an $N \times N$ matrix representing the Web graph, where N is the number of Web pages in the graph. If page v has a link to page u, then let the matrix entry $M[u, v]$ be $1/|F_v|$. If there is no link from page v to page u, then $M[u, v]$

= 0. Let R_i be an $N \times 1$ vector representing the rank vector of the N pages after the i-th iteration. Then Formula (1.4) can be expressed as:

$$R_i = M * R_{i-1} \tag{1.5}$$

where R_0 is the initial rank vector with all entries having value $1/N$. When the ranks converge, the rank vector is the eigenvector of the matrix M with the corresponding eigenvalue being 1. Note that if every page has at least one forward link, then the sum of the values in each column of M is 1 and all values are non-negative (such a matrix is called a *stochastic matrix*). Looking from a different angle, the entries of matrix M can be interpreted as follows. Consider a surfer who is surfing the Web. At each step, the surfer follows a random link from the current page to one of its child pages. Thus, the value at entry $M[u, v]$ can be interpreted as the probability that a random walk from page v to its child pages will lead to page u.

Now consider the effect on the ranks of pages by applying Formula (1.5). Suppose page v has a number of child pages. When Formula (1.5) is applied, the rank of v is propagated to its children. If each page has at least one forward link, the ranks of all pages will be passed on to their children. Since the sum of the ranks of all pages is initially 1, the sum is preserved after each iteration. Suppose by repeatedly applying Formula (1.5), the ranks of the pages converge. The converged rank of a page can be interpreted as the probability that the page will be visited by a random walk on the Web graph.

There is a problem with using the Formula (1.5) directly. That is, the ranks are guaranteed to converge only if M is *aperiodic* (i.e., the Web graph is not a single large cycle) and *irreducible* (i.e., the Web graph is *strongly connected*) (Haveliwala, T., 1999; Motwani and Raghavan, 1995). While the former (i.e., aperiodicity) is practically guaranteed for the Web, the latter is usually not true. A directed graph is said to be strongly connected if for any two distinct vertices in the graph, there is a directed path from one vertex to the other and vice versa. When the Web graph is not strongly connected, there may be pages (or a set of pages involved in a cycle) that only have backlinks but no forward links. These pages, which can only receive rank propagation from their parents but cannot propagate ranks to other pages, are called *rank sink* (Page et al., 1998). The existence of rank sink can cause the loss of total rank value. One way to solve this problem is to conceptually add a link from each page to every page in the Web graph and associate an appropriate positive probability with each such a link (Haveliwala, T., 1999). The probabilities should be assigned in such a way that the matrix corresponding to the resulted Web graph has the stochastic property (i.e., the sum of all entries in each column is 1). Suppose a link is conceptually added from page v to page u with probability p. In the random walk model, this can be interpreted as that the Web surfer, while at page v, may jump to page u with probability p. Note that v and u may be the same page. In this case, the jump can be interpreted as a *refresh* or *reload* request using the Web browser.

Let us now consider how to assign probabilities to added links. Consider the following two cases for a given page v.

1. *Page v has no forward links in the original Web graph* In this case, the Web surfer can only follow one of the added links (i.e., can only jump). It is reasonable to assume that the Web surfer may jump to any page with the same probability. Therefore, each added link from page v should have the probability $1/N$. This is equivalent to making all the entries in the column corresponding to page v in the matrix be $1/N$.

2. *Page v has at least one forward link in the original Web graph,* i.e., $|F_v| \geq 1$. Based on matrix M, each such link is assigned a probability of $1/|F_v|$. This probability needs to be modified because without any change the probabilities for the newly added links can only be zero, indicating no jumps are possible. Let c be a weight parameter satisfying $0 < c < 1$. Then we may adjust the probability for each original link from $1/|F_v|$ to $c * 1/|F_v|$ while assign probability $(1 - c) * 1/N$ to each newly added link from v. The closer to 1 the value of c is, the smaller the impact of the added links will be. It is easy to see that the sum of these probabilities is 1.

Mathematically, the addition of the links, the assignment of the probabilities to newly added links, and the adjustment of the probabilities on original links can be done by modifying the matrix M to the following new matrix:

$$M^* = c * (M + Z) + (1 - c) * K \tag{1.6}$$

where Z is an $N \times N$ matrix such that all entries in the column corresponding to page v are either $1/N$, if v has no forward links in the original graph, or zero if v has at least one forward link; K is an $N \times N$ matrix with all entries having the value of $1/N$; and c is a constant between 0 an 1.

When matrix M in Formula (1.5) is replaced by the new matrix M^*, the problem associated with rank sinks will be solved. Efficient techniques for computing PageRanks exist (Haveliwala, T., 1999)

Finally, after convergence, the PageRanks of pages can be normalized by dividing the PageRank of each page by the maximum PageRank of all pages so that the normalized PageRank of any page is between 0 and 1. In this case, a page with PageRank = 1 is considered to be the most important document and a page with PageRank = 0 is considered to be least important.

Example 1.3 Consider the directed graph in Fig 1.4. Suppose nodes in the graph correspond to Web pages and directed edges denote links. We now compute the rank of each page.

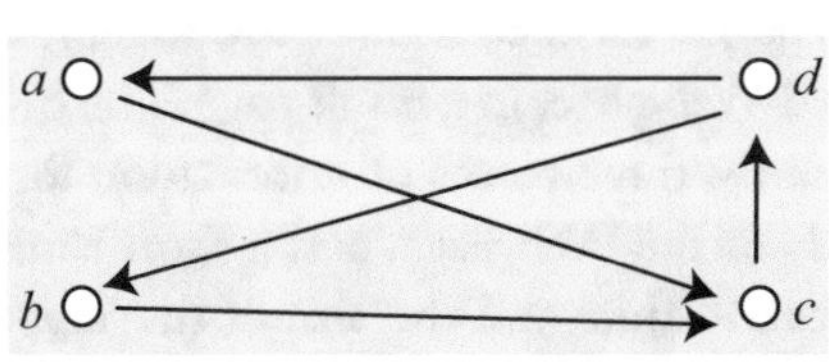

Figure 1.4: A Sample Web Graph.

Based on the graph in Fig. 1.4, we have

$$M = \begin{bmatrix} 0 & 0 & 0 & 1/2 \\ 0 & 0 & 0 & 1/2 \\ 1 & 1 & 0 & 0 \\ 0 & 0 & 1 & 0 \end{bmatrix}.$$

Since each node has at least one forward link, all entries in matrix Z are zero. Since there are four vertices, all entries in matrix K are 1/4. Suppose the constant c in Formula (1.6) is 0.8. Then the new matrix M^* is as follows:

$$M^* = 0.8 * (M + Z) + 0.2 * K = \begin{bmatrix} 0.05 & 0.05 & 0.05 & 0.45 \\ 0.05 & 0.05 & 0.05 & 0.45 \\ 0.85 & 0.85 & 0.05 & 0.05 \\ 0.05 & 0.05 & 0.85 & 0.05 \end{bmatrix}.$$

Suppose all pages have the same initial rank of 0.25, i.e., $R_0 = (0.25, 0.25, 0.25, 0.25)_t$, where V_t denotes the transpose of vector V. After 30 iterations, we obtain the following converged PageRanks $R(a) = R(b) = 0.176$, $R(c) = 0.332$ and $R(d) = 0.316$. Note that page c is pointed to by 2 pages, while each of the other pages is pointed to by 1 page only. As a result, the PageRank of c is higher than that of other pages. The reason why the rank of d is higher than that of page a or that of page b is that d is pointed at by the most important page, namely page c.

PageRank is computed based on link information alone, and the contents of the Web pages are not considered. As a result, they must be used together with content-based similarity (the similarities discussed in Section 1.2.3 are content-based similarities as they are computed based on the contents of the query and documents) for search engines to retrieve important and relevant Web pages for each query.

1.3.5 RESULT ORGANIZATION

Most search engines organize retrieved results in descending order of their estimated desirability with respect to a given query. The *desirability* of a page to a query could be approximated in many different ways such as the similarity of the page with the query or a combined measure including the similarity and PageRank of the page. A related issue is how to represent a *search result record* (SRR), which corresponds to a retrieved Web page, in a result page. The SRRs generated by most popular search engines consist of, primarily, three pieces of information for each retrieved Web page: the title of the Web page, the URL of the Web page, and a short summary known as *snippet*. Other information such as the publication time and the size of the Web page are also included in the SRRs by some search engines. Sometimes, the title is a clickable text with the URL encoded. The snippet is usually a short descriptive text of about 20 words extracted from the Web page. It serves the purpose of providing more hint than the title about the content of the page so that the user can make a more informed decision on whether to view the full Web page. The snippet of a page is often a text segment of the page that starts a sentence and has a good concentration of the query terms.

Some search engines organize the results into groups such that pages that have certain common features, such as having similar content or from the same Web site, are placed into the same group. Such an organization of the results, when informative labels are given to each group, can make it easier for users to identify useful pages from the returned results, especially when the query has multiple interpretations and the number of results returned for a query is large. A well known example is the Yippy search engine (formerly known as Clusty; `http://search.yippy.com/`). It organizes returned results for each query into groups. Some of the issues that need to be addressed when implementing an online result-clustering algorithm include the following: (1) What information (titles, URLs, snippets versus the full documents) should be used to perform the clustering? While more information may improve the quality of the clusters, using too much information may cause long delays for users due to high computation and communication overhead. (2) What criteria should be used to perform clustering? It could be based on the similarity between SSRs, i.e., results that are highly similar should be grouped together. It could also be based on the interpretation of the query, i.e., results that conform to the same interpretation should be grouped together. (3) How to come up with a short and yet meaningful label for each group? (4) How to organize the groups? They could be linearly ordered or hierarchically ordered. In the former case, what should be the linear order? In the latter case, how to generate the hierarchy? Some of the issues are still being actively researched.

There are also search engines that present the search results graphically so that the relationships between different results can be visualized. For example, the Liveplasma music and movie search engine (`http://www.liveplasma.com/`) displays the results as annotated icons that are grouped by some common features (e.g., movies with the same lead actor) and are connected by different links (e.g., one link connects to the director of a movie).

1.4 BOOK OVERVIEW

The rest of the book will focus on advanced metasearch engine technology. We now provide a brief overview of each of the remaining chapters.

Chapter 2 first provides an overview of the main components of a typical large-scale metasearch engine. These components include search engine selector, search engine incorporator, and result merger. Then this chapter will attempt to make a case for the metasearch engine technology as a viable alternative to major search engines based on a careful analysis of the advantages and disadvantages of both technologies. Finally, the Web environment in which metasearch engines will be built will be discussed to provide some insight to the challenges in building large-scale metasearch engines.

Chapter 3 focuses on the search engine selection component. The objective of this component is to determine which search engines, among the search engines used by a metasearch engine, have the best chance to return useful results for any given user query. Three important issues will be addressed in this chapter: how to represent the content of each search engine, how to use the representative information to make search engine selection, and how to generate the representative information.

Several types of approaches will be introduced with the emphasis on the type of approaches that use detailed statistics of search terms to represent the search engine content.

Chapter 4 discusses techniques that are needed to add search engines to a metasearch engine. Two main issues will be covered. The first is about establishing communication between a metasearch engine and each of its component search engines. Basically, a metasearch engine needs to pass user queries to each search engine, with necessary query reformatting according to the query format of each search engine, and receive the response page(s) returned by each search engine. The second issue is about extracting the search result records, each of which corresponds to one retrieved page, from the response pages. Several result extraction techniques will be introduced.

Chapter 5 introduces various result merging algorithms. These algorithms will cover a wide spectrum of scenarios along several dimensions. One dimension is the kinds of information regarding each result that are used to perform the merging, ranging from the local ranks of each result, to the title and snippet of each result, and to the full document of the result. Some merging algorithms use a combination of multiple types of information. A second dimension is the degree of overlap of documents among the search engines used to answer a query, ranging from no overlap, to some overlap, and to identical document collections.

Chapter 6 summarizes the main discussions of this book, discusses future directions for metasearch engine technology and lists a few specific remaining research challenges.

CHAPTER 2

Metasearch Engine Architecture

A metasearch engine is a search system that provides a unified way to access multiple existing search engines. It is based on the concept of *metasearch*, which is the paradigm of searching multiple data sources on the fly. Metasearch has a meaning very similar to *federated search*, and these two phrases are sometimes used interchangeably. A metasearch engine is sometimes also called a *search broker* because it acts as a "middleman" between users searching for information and a set of search engines (Craswell, N., 2000). Metasearch engine is also closely related to *distributed information retrieval* (Craswell, N., 2000) or *federated search system* (Shokouhi and Si, 2011) although there are some differences between them that will be discussed in Section 2.1.

The concept of metasearch on the Web has been around since early 1990s. One of the earliest, if not the earliest, metasearch engines is MetaCrawler (`http://www.metacrawler.com/`), which was first developed in 1994. Since then, a large number of metasearch engines have been developed and put in use on the Web. Some of these metasearch engines will be mentioned in this chapter and in subsequent chapters.

In this chapter, we will provide some general discussions about the metasearch engine technology. In Section 2.1, a reference metasearch engine architecture will be introduced. This architecture contains all the main system components and the function of each component will be described. In Section 2.2, an in-depth analysis of the advantages and disadvantages of the metasearch engine technology in comparison to the search engine technology will be provided. This analysis aims to make a convincing argument that the metasearch engine technology and, especially large-scale metasearch engine technology, has nice unique features that search engines do not have, and it can play an important role in the increasingly important Web search landscape. In Section 2.3, we will provide a careful examination of the Web environment in which metasearch engines are built and operate. The goal of this examination is to shed some light on the reasons that make building metasearch engines, especially large-scale metasearch engines, difficult and challenging.

2.1 SYSTEM ARCHITECTURE

Metasearch engines that search text documents can be classified into two types – general-purpose metasearch engines and special-purpose metasearch engines. The former aims to search the entire Web, while the latter focuses on searching information in a particular domain (e.g., news, jobs).

There are two approaches to building each type of metasearch engines:

- **Major search engine approach**. This approach uses a small number of popular major search engines to build a metasearch engine. Thus, to build a general-purpose metasearch engine using this approach, we can use a small number of major search engines such as Google, Yahoo!, Bing (MSN) and Ask. Similarly, to build a special-purpose metasearch engine for a given domain, we can use a small number of major search engines in that domain. For example, for the news domain, Google News, Yahoo! News, Reuters, etc., can be used.

- **Large-scale metasearch engine approach**. In this approach, a large number of mostly small search engines are used to build a metasearch engine. For example, to build a general-purpose metasearch engine using this approach, we can perceivably utilize all document-driven search engines on the Web. Such a metasearch engine will have millions of component search engines. Similarly, to build a special-purpose metasearch engine for a given domain with this approach, we can connect to all the search engines in that domain. For instance, for the news domain, tens of thousands of newspaper and news-site search engines can be used.

Each of the above two approaches has its advantages and disadvantages, and these will be detailed throughout this section. An obvious advantage of the major search engine approach is that such a metasearch engine is much easier to build compared to the large-scale metasearch engine approach because the former only requires the metasearch engine to interact with a small number of search engines. Almost all currently popular metasearch engines, such as Dogpile (`http://www.dogpile.com/`), Mamma (`http://www.mamma.com/`) and MetaCrawler (`http://www.metacrawler.com/`), are built using the major search engine approach, and most of them use only a handful of major search engine. One example of a large-scale special-purpose metasearch engine is AllInOneNews (`http://www.allinonenews.com/`), which uses about 1,800 news search engines from about 200 countries/regions. In general, more advanced technologies are required to build large-scale metasearch engines. As these technologies become more mature, more large-scale metasearch engines are likely to be built.

When designing metasearch engine system architecture, we should take both approaches into consideration. The architecture shown in Fig. 2.1 is based on this consideration. Significant software components included in this architecture include *search engine selector*, *search engine incorporator* and *result merger*. The search engine incorporator has two subcomponents: *search engine connector* and *result extractor*. Search engines used in a metasearch engine will be called *component search engines* of the metasearch engine in this book.

We now provide more detailed description about each of the main metasearch engine components shown in Fig. 2.1.

Search engine selector: If the number of component search engines in a metasearch engine is very small, say less than 10, it might be reasonable to send each user query submitted to the metasearch engine to all the component search engines. In this case, the search engine selector is probably not needed. However, if the number of component search engines is large, as in the large-scale metasearch engine scenario, then sending each query to all component search engines will be an inefficient strategy because most component search engines will be useless with respect to any particular query. For example, suppose a user wants to find 50 best matching

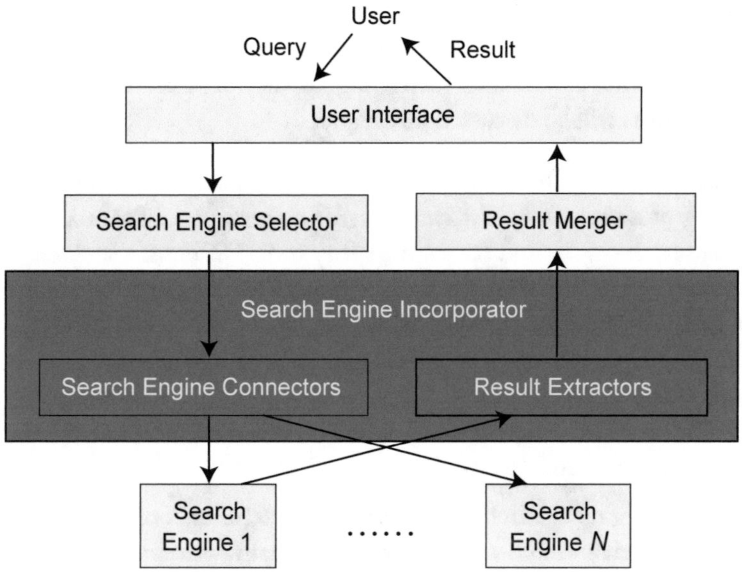

Figure 2.1: Metasearch Engine System Architecture.

results for his/her query from a metasearch engine with 1,000 component search engines. Since the 50 best results will be contained in no more than 50 component search engines, it is clear that at least 950 component search engines are useless for this particular query.

Passing a query to useless search engines may cause serious problems for efficiency. Generally, sending a query to useless search engines will cause waste of resources to the metasearch engine server, each of the involved search engine servers and the Internet. Specifically, dispatching a query, including needed query reformatting, to a useless search engine and handling the returned results, including receiving the returned response pages, extracting the result records from these pages, and determining whether they should be included in the final merged result list and where they should be ranked in the merged result list if they are to be included, waste the resources of the metasearch engine server; receiving the query from the metasearch engine, evaluating the query, and returning the results back to the metasearch engine waste the resources of each search engine whose results end up useless; and finally transmitting a query from the metasearch engine to useless search engines and transmitting useless retrieved results from these search engines to the metasearch engine waste the network resources of the Internet.

Therefore, it is important to send each user query to only potentially useful search engines for processing. The problem of identifying potentially useful component search engines to invoke for a given query is the *search engine selection problem*, which is sometimes also referred to as *database selection problem*, *server selection problem*, or *query routing problem*. Obviously, for metasearch engines with more component search engines and/or more diverse component search engines, having an effective search engine selector is more important. Search engine selection techniques will be discussed in Chapter 3.

Search engine connectors: After a component search engine has been selected to participate in the processing of a user query, the *search engine connector* establishes a connection with the server of the search engine and passes the query to it. Different search engines usually have different connection parameters. As a result, a separate connector is created for each search engine. In general, the connector for a search engine *S* needs to know the HTTP (HyperText Transfer Protocol) connection parameters supported by *S*. There are three basic parameters, (a) the name and location of the search engine server, (b) the HTTP request method (usually it is either GET or POST) supported by *S*, and (c) the name of the string variable that is used to hold the actual query string.

When implementing metasearch engines with a small number of component search engines, the connector for each search engine can be manually written by experienced developers. However, for large-scale metasearch engines, this can be very time-consuming and expensive. Thus, it is important to develop the capability of generating connectors automatically.

Note that an intelligent metasearch engine may modify a query it receives from a user before passing it to the search engine connector if such a modification can potentially improve the search effectiveness. For example, a query expansion technique may be used by the metasearch engine to add terms that are related to the original user query to improve the chance for retrieving more relevant documents.

Search engine connectors will be discussed in Chapter 4.

Result extractors: After a query is processed by a component search engine, one or more response pages will be returned by the search engine. A typical response page contains multiple (usually 10) *search result records* (SRRs), each of which corresponds to a retrieved Web page, and it typically contains the URL and the title of the page, a short summary (called *snippet*) of the page content, and some other pieces of information such as the page size. Fig. 2.2 shows the upper portion of a response page from the Google search engine. Response pages are dynamically generated HTML documents, and they often also contain content unrelated to the user query such as advertisements (sponsored links) and information about the host Web site.

A program (i.e., *result extractor*) is needed to extract the correct SRRs from each response page so that the SRRs from different component search engines can be merged into a single ranked list. This program is sometimes called an *extraction wrapper*. Since different search engines often format their results differently, a separate result extractor is usually needed for each component search engine. Although experienced programmers can write the extractors

Figure 2.2: A Portion of a Response Page from Google.

manually, for large-scale metasearch engines, it is desirable to develop techniques that can generate the extractors automatically.

Result extraction techniques will be discussed in Chapter 4.

Result merger: After the results from the selected component search engines are returned to the metasearch engine, the *result merger* combines the results into a single ranked list. The ranked list of SRRs is then presented to the user, possibly 10 records on each page at a time, just like most search engines do.

Many factors may influence how result merging will be performed and what the outcome will look like. Some of these factors are as follows: (1) How much overlap is there among the document collections indexed by different component search engines? The possibilities range from no overlap to identical document collections, and to anywhere in between the two extremes. (2) What kinds of information are available or can be used to perform the merging? The information that could be utilized includes the local rank of a result record from a component search engine, the title and the snippet of a result record, the full document of each result, the publication time of each retrieved document, the potential relevance of the search engine with respect to the query from where a result is retrieved, and more. A good result merger should rank all returned results in descending order of their desirability.

Different methods for performing result merging will be discussed in Chapter 5.

2.2 WHY METASEARCH ENGINE TECHNOLOGY?

In this section, we attempt to provide a comprehensive analysis of the potential advantages of metasearch engines over search engines. We will focus on the comparison of general-purpose metasearch engines and general-purpose search engines.

Increased Search Coverage. By providing a unified access to all the component search engines, a metasearch engine can search any document that is indexed by at least one of the component search engines. Hence, the search coverage of a metasearch engine is the union of those of its component search engines. This benefit is the main motivation behind early metasearch engines, and this is still their most recognized benefit.

In Section 2.1, we described two possible approaches to implement general-purpose metasearch engines, i.e., the *major search engine approach* and the *large-scale metasearch engine approach*. The phrase "increased search coverage" has somewhat different meanings for these two approaches. For the former, it can be viewed from two aspects. First, it is widely accepted and strongly supported by evidence that different major search engines index different sets of Web pages even though they all try to index the entire Web. This means that a metasearch engine with multiple major search engines as components will have larger coverage than any single component search engine. Second, different search engines often employ different document representation and result ranking techniques, and as a result, they often return different sets of top results for the same user query. A study based on 19,332 user queries showed that the overlap of the first page search results from all the four major search engines Google, Yahoo!, MSN and Ask was only 0.6% on average for each query[2] (Dogpile.com, 2007). Thus, by retrieving from multiple major search engines, a metasearch engine is likely to return more unique high quality results for each user query.

For the large-scale metasearch engine approach, due to the use of specialized component search engine, overlap across different component search engines is less likely. As a result, the combined coverage of such type of metasearch engine will be many times larger than the coverage of any single search engine. In fact, if all specialized document-driven search engines, including those that search the deep Web, can be included in a single large-scale metasearch engine, then this metasearch engine is likely to have much larger coverage than any major search engine or metasearch engine built based on the major search engine approach, because major search engines lack sufficient deep Web coverage. In this book, we will call this yet-to-be-built metasearch engine the WebScales metasearch engine because WebScales is the name of a project that systematically investigated the issues related to building large-scale metasearch engines (`http://www.cs.binghamton.edu/~meng/metasearch.html`[3]).

Easier to Reach the Deep Web. As we mentioned in Chapter 1, the Web consists of two parts – the surface Web and the deep Web, and the size of the deep Web is much larger than that

[2]In this study, a result is considered as an overlap if it is retrieved by all the four search engines.
[3]Accessed on November 3, 2010.

of the surface Web. Major search engines obtain their contents relying largely on traditional Web crawlers that fetch Web pages by following URL links. These crawlers can only reach the contents in the surface Web, which means that major search engines primarily cover the surface Web. In recent years, *deep Web crawlers* that can obtain deep Web contents are being developed and have achieved some success (Madhavan et al., 2008). Deep Web crawling is basically accomplished by submitting queries to deep Web search engines and gathering information from the returned results (Raghavan and Garcia-Molina, 2001; Madhavan et al., 2008). The main limitation of this technique is that it is very difficult to obtain the complete contents from deep Web search engines because it is almost impossible to use a reasonable number of queries to retrieve all the contents from a deep Web search engine.

Similar to deep Web crawlers, metasearch engines interact with search engines, including deep Web search engines, through their query interfaces (including APIs). But unlike deep Web crawlers, metasearch engines pass each user query directly to search engines to retrieve contents that are related to that query only, and there is no need to obtain the whole content of any search engine in advance. Since interacting with the query interface of a surface Web search engine is basically the same as that of a deep Web search engine, it is rather natural for metasearch engines to reach the deep Web. In summary, it is much easier for metasearch engines to reach the deep Web than major search engines.

It is clear that while general-purpose metasearch engines built using the major search engine approach will have the same difficulty in reaching the deep Web as major search engines do, it is the metasearch engine's approach of reaching a search engine's content directly through its query interface that makes it easier for metasearch engines to reach the deep Web.

Better Content Quality. The quality of the content of a search engine can be measured by the quality of the documents indexed by the search engine. The quality of a document can in turn be measured in a number of ways such as the richness and the reliability of the content. It is not the objective of this book to discuss the content quality formally. Instead, we offer some general analyses to support the argument that metasearch engines with specialized search engines as component search engines are more likely to reach better quality content than major search engines do. The analyses are based on the way major search engines gather Web pages and the way metasearch engine access search engine content.

Major search engines crawl documents from the open Web that contains both high quality documents (serious documents with useful contents) and poor quality documents because everyone can publish, and often anonymously, on the Web. Due to the huge number of Web documents (about 35 billion for Google) crawled, it is extremely difficult for these search engines to guarantee the quality of the crawled documents. As a result, poor quality results may be returned by major search engines. In contrast, specialized search engines are more likely to contain better quality documents because they often have more control on their contents. For example, many specialized search engines use only documents that they own or that come from trusted sources such as the search engines operated by newspapers and publishers where the contents are usually written by professional writers or contracted authors with editorial control. As large-scale metasearch engines use only specialized search engines as their component search engines, the contents they can search should also have better quality.

Major search engines rely on their crawlers to collect documents from numerous Web servers. However, these crawlers cannot keep up with the fast changing Web contents due to the huge numbers of Web pages and Web servers involved, as well as the constantly changing nature of the Web. It typically takes from several days to couple of weeks for newly updated or added contents to be crawled or re-crawled. Consequently, the contents indexed by major search engines are usually several days out-of-date on average. In contrast, it is much easier for specialized search engines to maintain the freshness of their contents because they use much smaller document collections and their contents are often stored on local servers. Therefore, general-purpose metasearch engines implemented using the large-scale metasearch engine approach has a better chance to retrieve more up-to-date information than major search engines and metasearch engines that are built with major search engines.

Good Potential for Better Retrieval Effectiveness. As we pointed out previously, there are two ways to create general-purpose metasearch engines. Each type of metasearch engine offers unique potential to achieve better retrieval effectiveness than major search engines.

There are two main reasons for a metasearch engine built using the major search engine approach to perform better than major search engines:

(1) More unique results are likely to be obtained, even among those highly ranked ones (Dogpile.com, 2007), due to the fact that different major search engines have different coverage and different document ranking algorithms.

(2) The result merging component of the metasearch engine can produce better results by taking advantage of the fact that the document collections of major search engines have significant overlaps. This means that many shared documents have the chance to be ranked by different search engines for any given query. If the same document is retrieved by multiple search engines, then the likelihood that the document is relevant to the query increases significantly because there is more evidence to support its relevance. In general, if a document is retrieved by more search engines, the document is more likely to be relevant based on the following important observation (Lee, J., 1997): Different search systems tend to retrieve the same set of relevant documents but different sets of irrelevant documents. Even though this observation was made based on applying different ranking algorithms to the same set of documents, it is still applicable when the document collections of different search engines have a high degree of overlap. The effectiveness of combining multiple evidences from different retrieval systems in text retrieval has been well established and an excellent survey on this topic can be found in (Croft, W., 2000).

For a metasearch engine built using the large-scale metasearch engine approach, due to the use of specialized component search engines, the degree of overlap among the document collections of the selected component search engines for any particular query is likely to be very low. As a result, the aforementioned combining approach cannot be utilized. However, there are a number of other reasons why such a metasearch engine may achieve better effectiveness than major search engines. We discuss these reasons below.

(1) As mentioned above, the document collections of specialized search engines likely have better quality than those of major search engines and the combined coverage of these search engines is higher than any major search engine. This provides the basis for the metasearch engine to perform better than any major search engine.

(2) Some specialized search engines utilize domain knowledge (e.g., domain specific ontology and semantic dictionary) to improve retrieval effectiveness. By using these search engines to perform the search, the metasearch engine can take advantage of their special capabilities while major search engines cannot.

(3) A typical large-scale metasearch engine has a three-step process to zoom in on the best results for each query. First, the search engine selector identifies the search engines that are most likely to return relevant results for the given query and only these search engines will be invoked for this query. Second, each selected search engine returns to the metasearch engine the best results based on its ranking algorithm. Finally, the result merger of the metasearch engine identifies the best overall results from the best local results returned by the search engines that have the best match with the given user query. With a high quality search engine selection algorithm, high quality component search engines and a high quality result merging method, this three-step process has the potential to produce very high quality results for any user query.

Better utilization of resources. Metasearch engines use component search engines to perform basic search. This allows them to utilize the storage and computing resources of these search engines. As a result, they avoid the following expenses that are needed for running a search engine: (1) crawling and storing the document collection, (2) indexing collected documents, and (3) searching the index database. For large search engines, just the cost of purchasing the needed computers, housing them, and maintaining their operations (including software/hardware maintenance and power consumption) can be very high. Although metasearch engines also need their own infrastructure to perform their functionalities such as search engine selection, representative generation, and result merging, their requirement for infrastructure is much less compared to that for search engines of the same scale.

While large-scale metasearch engines have the above advantages over major search engines, they also have some inherent disadvantages. First, it will take longer for a metasearch engine to return results to its user than major search engines do because a metasearch engine has to pass each query to the selected component search engines, wait for the query to be processed by them, and finally wait for the results to be returned from them. Major search engines take less than a second to evaluate a query while metasearch engines often take 2-5 seconds to return results. Much of the difference can be attributed to the added network communication between the metasearch engine and its component search engines when a query is evaluated by a metasearch engine. This difference in response time between search engines and metasearch engines is likely to reduce in the future with increased speed of the Internet. Second, major search engines have full control of their document ranking algorithms and have a better chance to utilize the link information among Web pages. In contrast, metasearch engines have no control of the component search engines and are at the mercy of these search engines. The response time, quality of the results, and the quality of the result snippets of these search engines can significantly impact the performance of the metasearch engine. In addition, specialized search engines do not have the global link graph and, as a result, will not be able to utilize this graph in their ranking functions. A study (Wang and DeWitt, 2004) indicates that it is possible to estimate the global PageRank of a page from a component search engine by adjusting the local PageRank of the page computed based on the links among Web pages within the search engine using the PageRanks of the search engines (called ServerRanks). ServerRanks are computed using the links between the hosting sites of the search engines. However, to compute ServerRanks accurately, inter-server links that appear in the pages of a search engine need to be made available to the metasearch engine.

Another potential problem for metasearch engines is that some search engines may not want to be used as component search engines of metasearch engine for two reasons. First, queries from metasearch engines will consume the resources of search engines. Second, it may reduce the number of user visits to the search engines, which may in turn reduce advertisement revenue of the search engines. These reasons are significant only for popular search engines with steady advertisement revenue. Google is an example of such a search engine that prohibits queries from metasearch engines unless they sign an agreement with Google in advance. In contrast, specialized search engines have little motivation to block queries from metasearch engines because they are often less well-known, have limited query traffic, and do not rely on advertisement to make money. Many of them just sell content and services, and many others have the main goal of information dissemination. In fact, there is strong incentive for them to participate in metasearch engines because the latter can help these search engines reach more users and gain more recognition (metasearch engines usually identify, for each result displayed, the search engine that retrieved it).

The above discussions suggest that search engines and metasearch engines are complementary approaches for Web search engine. A single search system that can take advantage of both approaches may ultimately be the best solution. In such a system, each user query is processed by a major search engine and a large-scale metasearch engine. The former can return results from the surface Web quickly; while the user is going through these results, the latter can potentially retrieve more and better results for the user.

As we have discussed before, there are significant technical challenges in building very large-scale metasearch engines like WebScales. Although much research is still needed, a lot of progress has already been made. In the next three chapters, some of these progresses will be reported.

2.3 CHALLENGING ENVIRONMENT

For the most part, the component search engines that are used by metasearch engines are autonomous, i.e., they are built and maintained independently. The developers of each search engine decide what documents the search engine will provide search services to, how documents should be represented, and when the index should be updated. Similarities between documents and user queries are computed using a similarity function. It is again up to the developers of each search engine to decide what similarity function to use. Developers of commercial search engines often regard the similarity functions they use and other implementation details as proprietary information, and they do not make them available to the general public. In general, metasearch engines need to interact with search engines without their direct cooperation.

As a direct consequence of the autonomy of component search engines, a number of heterogeneities exist. In Section 2.3.1, we identify major heterogeneities that are unique in the metasearch engine environment and discuss their impact on metasearch engine construction. Heterogeneities that are common to other autonomous systems (e.g., multidatabase systems) such as different operating system platforms will not be described. In Section 2.3.2, we provide a brief review of some efforts that aim to ease the interaction between a metasearch engine and its component search engines.

2.3.1 HETEROGENEITIES AND THEIR IMPACT

The following heterogeneities can be identified among autonomous component search engines (Meng et al., 1999b, 2002).

1. *Document Collection.* The document collection of different search engines may differ at two levels. The first level is the topic or subject area of a collection. For example, one collection may contain medical documents and another may contain legal documents. In this case, the two collections are on different topics. In practice, the topic area of a collection may not be easily determined as some may contain documents from multiple areas. The second level is the actual documents. Even when two collections are on the same topic, they can still have totally different sets of documents. In general, the relationships among multiple document collections can be complicated because at both the topic level and the document level, they can have different degrees of overlaps.

2. *Query Language.* Each search engine supports a pre-defined set of query models, ranging from vector space model, Boolean model and proximity model to exact string match and numeric range match. Furthermore, different search engines often support different sets of query models, use different notations to represent the same operators, and have different default interpretations for user submitted keyword queries containing no explicit operators.

3. *Server Connection.* Unlike human users who submit queries to a search engine through an interface on a Web browser, a metasearch engine does so by sending queries to the search engine server directly. Each search engine has a connection configuration, which needs to be used by any application to connect with it. A typical configuration contains the name and the Internet location of the server, the HTTP request method supported, the query string name, and a number of default query string name and value pairs (please see Chapter 4 for more details). Different search engines usually have different connection configurations.

4. *Response Page Format.* All search engines present their retrieved results in dynamically-generated response pages in HTML-coded format. Such a format is usually pre-designed and is known as a *template.* A template may contain multiple sections, for example, one section for showing the search result records and another for displaying the sponsored links. Within each section, the template controls how the information in the section should be organized and displayed. The response page as well as the section that contains the search result records usually has very different templates across different search engines.

5. *Indexing Method.* Different search engines may employ different techniques to determine the terms that are used to represent a given document. For example, some search engines use only terms that appear in a Web page to index the Web page, but many search engines also use the *anchor terms* that appear in other Web pages to index the referenced Web page. Other examples of different indexing techniques include whether or not to remove *stop words*, whether or not to perform *stemming*, and whether or not to recognize phrasal terms. Furthermore, different stop word lists and different stemming algorithms may be used, and different phrases may be recognized by different search engines.

6. *Term Weighting Scheme.* Different schemes can be used to determine the weight of a term in a Web page. For example, one method uses the *term frequency weight* and another uses the product of the *term frequency weight* and the *inverse document frequency weight* (see Section 1.2.2). Several variations of these schemes exist (Salton, G., 1989). Some search engines also take the location and/or font of a term occurrence into weight computation. For example, the weight of a term may be increased if it appears in the title of a Web page or if its font is boldface (more discussion on this can be found in Section 1.3.3).

7. *Similarity Function.* Different search engines may employ different similarity functions to measure the degree of match between a query and a Web page. Some popular similarity functions for text documents were described in Section 1.2.3, including *Cosine function* and *Okapi function.* In Section 1.3.4, we also discussed that link-derived importance (e.g., PageRank) can also be incorporated into a similarity function. In practice, a large number of factors may be considered by a similarity function, and the ranking formula can become very complicated. For example, it was reported that more than 250 factors were taken into consideration by Google's ranking formula in 2008 (Hiemstra, D., 2008).

8. *Document Version*. Individual documents on the Web may be modified anytime by their authors or even automatically by some software. Typically, when a Web page is modified, those search engines that indexed the Web page will not be notified of the modification. Before a search engine can re-fetch and re-index a modified Web page, the representation of the Web page in the search engine is based on a stale or out-dated version of the page. Due to the huge size of the Web, Web crawlers of large search engines can only afford to revisit their previously indexed pages periodically (from days to weeks). As a result, between two visits by a search engine's crawler, a page may experience multiple changes. Since search engines are autonomous, their crawlers may fetch or re-fetch the same page[4] at different times. Consequently, it is highly likely that different search engines may have indexed different versions of the same page at any given time.

The autonomy and heterogeneities discussed above have profound impact on the construction of each main component of metasearch engines. We discuss these below.

1. *On Search Engine Selection*. First, the fact that different component search engines have different document collections is the basis for the need of search engine selection. Second, in order to estimate the usefulness of a search engine to a given query, the *search engine selector* needs to have some knowledge about the contents of the search engine's document collection. We call the knowledge that summarizes the contents of a search engine's document collection as the *content representative*, or simply *representative*, of the search engine. Key challenges in developing effective search engine selection algorithms are as follows: (1) How to summarize the contents of a search engine's document collection? In other words, what kind of a representative should be used? (2) How to use the representatives of different component search engines to perform selection? (3) How to generate the desired representatives? The last issue is made more difficult if component search engines are not cooperative in providing the information needed by the representatives. Due to the autonomy of search engines, their cooperation is often not possible. In Chapter 3, we will examine each of the above three issues in detail.

2. *On Search Engine Incorporation*. As discussed in Section 2.1, the search engine incorporator component consists of two subcomponents: *query dispatcher* and *result extractor*. The query dispatcher in turn contains two programs for each component search engine, one is a *connection program* and one is a *query translator*. Clearly, the heterogeneities in server connection, query language and response page format across different component search engines have a direct impact on connection programs, query translators, and result extractors. Specifically, an individualized connection program, query translator and result extractor are needed for each component search engine. This makes developing large-scale metasearch engines much more challenging because it may no longer be practical to implement the huge number of connection programs, query translators, and result extractors manually. In Chapter 4, highly automated solutions to these subcomponents will be introduced.

[4] Each page is identified by its URL.

3. *Result merging*. Many factors influence the similarity between a document and a query and these factors include document collection (i.e., it affects the document frequency of each term and thus each term's *idf* weight), indexing method, term weighting scheme, similarity function and document version. The heterogeneities in these factors across different component search engines make the similarities computed by different search engines (with respect to the same query) not directly comparable. This means that the result merger should not directly use these similarities to rank the results returned from different search engines even if they were available. Modern search engines typically do not return the similarities of retrieved results, but these similarities are used internally to determine the ranks of the retrieved results. This implies that the local ranks of the retrieved results returned by different search engines are also not directly comparable. Such incomparability complicates the design of effective result merging algorithms. In Chapter 5, different result merging techniques will be presented.

2.3.2 STANDARDIZATION EFFORTS

As discussed in Section 2.3.1, the autonomy and the heterogeneities among different search engines make building metasearch engines very difficult. There have been substantial effort in the metasearch community to standardize the communication between metasearch engines and search engines so as to simplify the task of building metasearch engines. In this subsection, we provide a brief summary of some of the main efforts.

- STARTS (Stanford Proposal for Internet Meta-Searching) (Gravano et al., 1997). This is one of the earliest attempts to propose a protocol between search engines and metasearch engines. It considered how to support search engine selection, query mapping and result merging. For search engine selection, it requires a search engine to provide information about its word vocabulary (including stop words, stemming, case sensitivity, fields association) and some specific statistics (total term frequency in a search engine, document frequency and the number of documents in a search engine). It also requires an abstract (text description) of the content to be provided. STARTS had good discussion on query language issues, including keywords based query, Boolean operators, and proximity conditions. These are important for mapping metasearch engine queries to search engine queries. However, STARTS did not cover how search results should be formatted for easy extraction by metasearch engines.
- OpenSearch (`http://www.opensearch.org/Home`[5]). OpenSearch is developed by Amazon.com, and it supports the specification of some basic connection information (e.g., the location of the search engine server, the character encoding protocol and the language of the input), privacy information (e.g., whether the results can be displayed to the user or sent to other application), and high level content information (e.g., whether it has adult content). However, it generally does not support the specification of detailed search result format. Its "response element" supports some XML protocols such as RSS 2.0.

[5] Accessed on November 3, 2010.

- SRU (Search/Retrieval via URL; `http://www.loc.gov/standards/sru/`[6]) [SRU]. SRU can be considered as a special version of Z39.50 specifically tailored to make it more relevant to the Web environment. It specifies search engine location, query parameters, and result format using augmented URL with some details included in additional files. Each search engine supporting the SRU protocol should have an "explain record" that provides information about its capabilities such as search engine connection information.

  SRU has a query language called CQL (Common Query Language). CQL supports keywords searches, Boolean operations, and proximity conditions. The SRU protocol simplifies the interaction between any application and search engines, and therefore can be utilized to build metasearch engines. However, this protocol requires no or little information to facilitate search engine selection and result merging.

- MXG (Metasearch XML Gateway) (Standards Committee BC/Task Group 3, 2006). This is a standard developed by NISO (National Information Standards Organization). MXG is developed based on SRU for metasearch applications. It provides a mechanism for content providers to expose their content and services to metasearch engines. MXG has three levels of compliance, and a higher level compliance supports more interoperability and functionality. Level 1 requires a search engine to satisfy basic URL request compliance and response compliance (results are returned in XML format). But the metasearch engine developers need to figure out what capabilities each search engine has and how to convert its users' queries to the search engine's native query format. Level 2 further requires a search engine to provide additional information such as host server name, port number, and data collection name. Level 3 adds the requirement that each compliant search engine supports a standard query language – the Common Query Language. There isn't much difference between Level 3 MXG and SRU.

- NISO Metasearch Initiative (`http://www.niso.org/workrooms/mi/`[7]). NISO launched this initiative around the end of 2003. The MI Committee consists of three Task Groups. The first group focuses on access management (authentication and authorization). The second group focuses on collection description and service description. The third group focuses on search and retrieval. By the end of 2005, each task group published its recommendation/draft standard. MXG and SRU are both the products of the third group, and we have briefly mentioned them above.

  The second group produced two draft specifications in 2005, one for collection description (CD) (National Information Standards Organization, 2006a) and one for service description (SD) (National Information Standards Organization, 2006b). For CD, each collection has 28 properties (identifier, title, alternative title, description, size, language, type,

[6]Accessed on November 3, 2010.
[7]Accessed on November 3, 2010.

rights, access rights, accrual method, accrual periodicity, accrual policy, custodial history, audience, subject, spatial coverage, temporal coverage, accumulation date range, contents date range, subject completeness, collector, owner, is accessed via, sub-collection, super-collection, catalogue or description, associated collection, associated publication). The draft specification (National Information Standards Organization, 2006a) does not mention statistics about terms. For SD, information for describing a service includes location of the service, network protocol (e.g., HTTP), authentication or authorization protocol, means to access data (search, browse, sort, query language, fields/attributes, comparators), number of records that can be retrieved (or similar feature settings), etc.

NISO is part of ANSI (American National Standards Institute) and the MI effort involved participants from many organizations in the world. Thus, the proposed standards have some credibility. However, its current status is not clear because from the NISO MI Web site (`http://www.niso.org/workrooms/mi/`), it appears that the NISO MI committee has not been active since 2006.

Despite the above efforts, none of them is widely used to build real metasearch engines. Whether a single standard will emerge that will be widely embraced by search engine developers remains to be seen.

CHAPTER 3

Search Engine Selection

When a metasearch engine receives a query from a user, it invokes the *search engine selector* to select the component search engines to send the query to. Different possible criteria could be used as the basis to make the selection. For example, one possible criterion is the average response time of a search engine in response to user queries. In this book, we focus on content-based criteria, i.e., how well the content of a search engine's document collection match a query. A good search engine selection algorithm should identify potentially useful search engines for any given query accurately and rank them based on their estimated usefulness with the more useful ones ranked ahead of the less useful ones.

All search engine selection algorithms follow the following general methodology. First, they summarize the content of each search engine into its *content representative*. Second, when a user query comes, it is compared with the representatives of all search engines to estimate which search engines are most likely to return useful results to the query.

A large number of approaches have been proposed to tackle the search engine selection problem. These approaches differ in the representatives they use to summarize the content of each search engine's document collection, the measures they use to reflect the usefulness of each search engine with respect to a given query, and the algorithms they employ to estimate the usefulness. We classify these approaches into the following four categories[8].

1. **Rough representative approaches.** In these approaches, the content of a component search engine is often represented by a few selected keywords or paragraphs. Such a representative is only capable of providing a very general idea on what a search engine's content is about and, consequently, search engine selection algorithms using this type of representatives are not very accurate in estimating the true usefulness of search engines with respect to a given query. Rough representatives are often manually generated.

2. **Learning-based approaches.** In these approaches, the knowledge about which search engines are likely to return useful results to what types of queries is learned from past retrieval experiences. Such knowledge is then used to determine the usefulness of a search engine for new queries.

   The retrieval experiences could be obtained through the use of training queries before the search engine selection algorithm is put to use and/or through real user queries while search engine

[8]The first three categories were first used in (Meng et al., 2002).

selection is in active use. The experiences obtained about a search engine will be summarized as knowledge and saved as the representative of the search engine.

3. **Sample document-based approaches**. In these approaches, a set of sample documents from the document collection of each search engine is used as the representative of the search engine's content. For this type of approach to work well, it is important that the sampled documents from each search engine are sufficiently representative of the full document collection of the search engine.

4. **Statistical representative approaches**. These approaches usually represent the content of a search engine using rather detailed statistical information. Typically, the representative of a search engine contains some statistical information for each term in the search engine's document collection such as the *document frequency* of the term and the average weight of the term among all documents that contain it. Detailed statistics allow more accurate estimation of the usefulness of a search engine with respect to any user query. For large-scale metasearch engines, the scalability of such approaches is an important issue due to the amount of information that needs to be stored for each search engine.

Among these, statistical representative approaches are most popular and have received most attention. In this book, we will mostly focus on statistical representative approaches while providing a brief introduction to the other two types of approaches.

3.1 ROUGH REPRESENTATIVE APPROACHES

As mentioned earlier, a rough representative of a search engine uses only a few keywords or a few sentences to describe the content of the search engine. It is only capable of providing a very general idea on what the search engine's document collection is about.

In ALIWEB (Koster, M., 1994), the representative of a document collection is generated using a pre-defined template. The following is an example of the representative used to describe document collection for the Perl Programming Language:

```
Template-Type: DOCUMENT
Title: Perl
URI: /public/perl/perl.html
Description: Information on the Perl Programming Language.
             Includes a local Hypertext Perl Manual, and the
             latest FAQ in Hypertext.
Keywords: perl, perl-faq, language
Author-Handle: m.koster@nexor.co.uk
```

When determining how suitable document collections are for a user query, the collections are ranked based on how well their representatives match against the query. The match can be against one or more fields (e.g., title, description, etc.) of the representatives based on the user's choice. Note that ALIWEB was not a real metasearch engine because it only allowed users to select one collection to search at a time, and it performed no result merging. Descriptive content representatives were also used in WAIS (Kahle and Medlar, 1991), where more than one local collection can be searched at the same time.

In Search Broker (Manber and Bigot, 1997, 1998), one or two topic words are manually assigned to each search engine. Each user query consists of two parts: the subject part and the regular query part. When a query is received by the system, its subject part is used to identify the component search engines covering the same subject using the assigned topic words, and the regular query part is used to search documents from the identified search engines.

While most rough search engine representatives are generated with human involvement, automatically generated rough representatives exist. In Q-Pilot (Sugiura and Etzioni, 2000), each search engine is represented by a vector of terms with weights. The terms are obtained from the interface page of the search engine or from the pages that have links to the search engine. In the latter case, only terms that appear in the same line as the link to the search engine are used, and the weight of each term is the number of back link documents that contain the term.

The advantages of rough representative approaches include the relative ease with which representatives can be obtained and the little storage space that they require. Such an approach may work reasonably well when all component search engines are highly specialized and are on different topics because, in this case, it is relatively easy to summarize and differentiate the contents of these search engines. In other cases, this approach may be inadequate. To alleviate this problem, most such approaches involve users in the search engine selection process. For example, in ALIWEB and WAIS, users make the final decision as to which search engines (document collections) to select, based on the preliminary selections made by the system. In Search Broker, users are required to specify the subject areas for their queries. As users often do not know the component search engines well (especially when the number of component search engines is large), their involvement in the search engine selection process can easily miss useful search engines.

3.2 LEARNING-BASED APPROACHES

These approaches predict the usefulness of a search engine for new queries based on the retrieval results from past queries submitted to the search engine. The retrieval results can be summarized into useful knowledge for search engine selection. If the past queries are training queries, based on which the knowledge is obtained before the search engine selector is enabled, the corresponding approach is a *static learning approach* (Meng et al., 2002). The weakness of static learning is its inability to adapt to the changes in search engine content and user query patterns. If the past queries are real user queries and the knowledge is accumulated gradually and updated continuously, the corresponding approach is a *dynamic learning approach* (Meng et al., 2002). The problem with dynamic learning is that it may take a long time to accumulate enough knowledge for effective search engine selection. Static learning and dynamic learning can be combined to form a *combined-learning approach*. In such an approach, initial knowledge is obtained using training queries, but the knowledge is continuously updated based on real user queries. Combined-learning can overcome the weaknesses of the other two learning approaches. In this subsection, we introduce several learning based search engine selection methods.

An example of a static learning approach is the MRDD (Modeling Relevant Document Distribution) approach (Voorhees et al., 1995). In this approach, each training query is submitted to every component search engine. From the documents returned from a search engine for a given query, all relevant documents are identified, and a vector reflecting the distribution of the relevant documents is obtained and stored. Specifically, the vector has the format $< r_1, r_2, ..., r_s >$, where r_i is a positive integer indicating that r_i top-ranked documents must be retrieved from the search engine in order to obtain i relevant documents for the query. For example, suppose for a training query q and a search engine S, 50 results are retrieved and ranked. If the 1st, 3rd, 8th and 15th results are the only relevant ones, then the corresponding distribution vector is $< r_1, r_2, r_3, r_4 >=<1, 3, 8, 15>$.

After the vectors for all training queries and all search engines have been obtained, the search engine selector is ready to select search engines for user queries. When a user query is received, it is compared against all training queries, and the k most similar ones are identified for some integer k. Next, for each search engine S, the average relevant document distribution vector over the k vectors corresponding to the k most similar training queries for S is obtained. Finally, the average distribution vectors are used to select the search engines to invoke, and the documents to retrieve, by trying to maximize the precision for any given desired number of relevant documents.

Example 3.1 Suppose for a given user query q, the following three average distribution vectors are obtained for three search engines:

$$S_1 :< 1, 4, 6, 7, 10, 12, 17 >$$
$$S_2 :< 3, 5, 7, 9, 15, 20 >$$
$$S_3 :< 2, 3, 6, 9, 11, 16 >$$

Suppose we need to retrieve three relevant documents. To maximize the precision, we should retrieve one document from S_1 and three documents from S_3. In other words, search engines S_1 and S_3 should be selected. This selection yields a precision of 0.75 as three out of the four retrieved documents are relevant.

In the MRDD approach, the representative of a search engine is the set of distribution vectors for all the training queries. The main weakness of this approach is that learning has to be carried out manually for each training query. In addition, it may be difficult to identify appropriate training queries and the learned knowledge may become obsolete when the contents of the search engines experience significant change.

SavvySearch (Dreilinger and Howe, 1997) was a metasearch engine that employed the dynamic learning approach. It computes the ranking score of a search engine with respect to a query based on the retrieval performance of past queries that used the terms in the new query. More specifically, for each search engine S, a weight vector $(w_1, \ldots, w_m)$ is maintained by the search engine selector, where each w_i corresponds to term t_i in search engine S. Initially, all weights are zero. When a k-term query containing term t_i is submitted to search engine S, the weight w_i is adjusted according to the retrieval result as follows. If no document is returned by S, w_i is reduced by $1/k$; if at least one returned document is clicked by the user, w_i is increased by $1/k$; otherwise (i.e., when some results are returned but no one is clicked by the user), w_i stays the same. Intuitively, a large positive w_i indicates that the search engine S responded well to term t_i in the past and a large negative w_i indicates that S responded poorly to t_i.

SavvySearch also tracks the recent performance of each search engine S in terms of h – the average number of results returned for the most recent five queries, and r – the average response time for the most recent five queries sent to S. If h is below a threshold, a penalty p_h for S is computed. Similarly, if r is greater than a threshold, a penalty p_r is computed.

For a new query q with terms $t_1, \ldots, t_k$, the ranking score of search engine S is computed as follows:

$$r(q, S) = \frac{\sum_{i=1}^{k} w_i \bullet \log(N/f_i)}{|S|} - (p_h + p_r) \tag{3.1}$$

where $\log(N/f_i)$ is the inverse search engine frequency weight of term t_i, N is the number of component search engines of the metasearch engine, f_i is the number of search engines having a positive weight for term t_i, and $|S|$ is the length of the weight vector of S defined as $\sqrt{\sum |w_j|}$, where the sum is over all terms that have appeared in previous queries.

The search engine representative in SavvySearch contains weights for only terms that have been used in previous queries. Moderate effort is needed to maintain the information. One weakness of SavvySearch is that it will not work well for new query terms or query terms that have been used only very few times. In addition, the user feedback process employed by SavvySearch is not rigorous and could easily lead to problems. Specifically, search engine users have the tendency to check out some top-ranked results for their queries, regardless of whether these results are actually useful. In other words, a click on a result may not be an accurate indicator that the result is relevant. As a result, the weight of a term for a search engine may not accurately indicate how well the search engine will respond to the term. This weakness may be remedied to some extent by taking into consideration the amount of the time a user has spent to view a document when determining whether the document represents a positive response for a query.

ProFusion (Gauch et al., 1996; Fan and Gauch, 1999) was a metasearch engine employing the combined learning approach. In ProFusion, the following 13 categories were utilized in the learning process: "Science and Engineering," "Computer Science," "Travel," "Medical and Biotechnology," "Business and Finance," "Social and Religion," "Society, Law and Government," "Animals and Environment," "History," "Recreation and Entertainment," "Art," "Music" and "Food." Each category is represented by a set of terms. For each category, a set of training queries is utilized to learn how well each search engine responds to queries in different categories. For a given category C and a given search engine S, each associated training query q is submitted to S. From the top 10 retrieved documents, relevant ones are identified. Then a score reflecting the performance of S with respect to q and C is computed as $c * \frac{\sum_{i=1}^{10} N_i}{10} * \frac{R}{10}$, where c is a constant; $N_i = 1/i$ if the i-th ranked document is relevant and $N_i = 0$ if the document is irrelevant; R is the number of relevant documents in the 10 results. Finally, the scores of all training queries associated with category C is averaged for search engine S, and this average is the *confidence factor* of S with respect to C. At the end of the training (i.e., static learning), there is a confidence factor for each search engine with respect to each of the 13 categories.

When a user query q is received by the metasearch engine, q is first mapped to the categories that contain at least one term in q. Then the search engines are ranked based on the sum of the confidence factors of each search engine with respect to the mapped categories. This sum is called the *ranking score* of the search engine for q. In ProFusion, the three search engines with the highest ranking scores are selected for invocation for a given query.

In ProFusion, retrieved documents are ranked based on the product of the local similarity of each document and the ranking score of the search engine that has retrieved the document. Let d from search engine S be the first document clicked by the user. If d is not the top ranked result, then the ranking score of S should be increased while the ranking scores of those search engines whose documents are ranked higher than d should be reduced. This dynamic learning process is carried out by proportionally adjusting the confidence factors of S in mapped categories. For example, if the ranking score of S, RS, is to be reduced by δ and the confidence factor of S for a mapped category is currently f, then f will be reduced by $(f/RS) * \delta$. This ranking score adjustment strategy tends to move d higher in the rank if the same query is processed in the future. The rationale behind this strategy is that if the ranking scores were perfect, then the top ranked result would be the first to be checked by the user.

ProFusion has the following weaknesses. First, the static learning part is still done mostly manually, i.e., selecting training queries and identifying relevant documents are carried out manually. Second, it assumes that component search engines return the similarities of retrieved documents. Today, most search engines do not return such similarities. Third, the higher ranked documents from the same search engine that retrieved the first clicked document will remain higher-ranked after the adjustment of confidence factors. This is a situation where the dynamic learning strategy does not help retrieve better documents for repeating queries. Fourth, the employed dynamic learning method seems to be too simplistic. For example, users' tendency to select the highest ranked result is not taken into consideration. One way to alleviate this problem is to use the first clicked document that was read for a significant amount of time.

3.3 SAMPLE DOCUMENT-BASED APPROACHES

In this section, we assume that for each component search engine a set of sample documents has already been obtained, and these documents are sufficiently representative of the document collection of the search engine. The issue of how to obtain such a set of sample documents will be discussed in Section 3.4.6.

We introduce the following notations in this section. For component search engine S_i, let $SD(S_i)$ denote the set of sample documents collected for S_i. Let *CSD* denote the *centralized sample document collection* containing the sample documents for all component search engines, that is, *CSD* = $\cup_i SD(S_i)$. Let *CD* denote the *centralized document collection* containing the documents from all component search engines. Note that *CD* is not materialized; it is used for ease of discussion. If each $SD(S_i)$ is a good representative of S_i, then *CSD* can be considered a good representative of *CD*. A text retrieval system is built based on *CSD* with the global similarity function of the metasearch engine.

Several methods have been proposed to perform search engine selection based on *CSD*. These methods usually also use the size of each component search engine (i.e., the number of documents it has). The basic idea of these methods is as follows. When a query q is received by the metasearch engine, the query is evaluated against *CSD* to compute the global similarities or the global ranks of the documents in *CSD* with respect to q. Then these global similarities or global ranks are used to estimate the usefulness of each search engine with respect to q based on the assumption that each sampled document from search engine S_i represents $|S_i|/|SD(S_i)|$ documents in S_i. Different search engine usefulness measures are often used in different methods. In this section, we introduce three of these methods. A more complete survey of sample document-based search engine selection methods has been provided recently by Shokouhi and Si (2011).

The ReDDE (*relevant document distribution estimation*) algorithm (Si and Callan, 2003b) first estimates the number of documents that are relevant to any given query in each search engine and then ranks the search engines in descending order of these estimated numbers. Let $RelN(S, q)$ denote the number of documents in search engine S that are relevant to query q. $RelN(S, q)$ can be computed by the following formula:

$$RelN(S, q) = \sum_{d \in S} \Pr(rel|d) \Pr(d|S)|S| \tag{3.2}$$

where $\Pr(rel|d)$ is the probability that a document from S is relevant to q, $\Pr(d|S)$ is the probability that d is selected from S, and $|S|$ is the number of documents in S. Based on the assumption that $SD(S)$ is representative of the documents in S, $RelN(S, q)$ can be estimated as follows:

$$RelN(S, q) \approx \sum_{d \in SD(S)} \Pr(rel|d) \Pr(d|SD(S))|S| \tag{3.3}$$

where the probability that a given document d is selected from $SD(S)$ is $1/|SD(S)|$. In order to estimate $RelN(S, q)$ using Formula (3.3), we need to estimate $\Pr(rel|d)$ – the probability that any given document in $SD(S)$ is relevant to q. This is a fundamental problem in information retrieval and there is no general solution to this problem. One possibility is to define $\Pr(rel|d)$ as the probability of relevance given d's rank among all documents in *CD* (the centralized document collection) based on the global similarities between these documents and q (Si and Callan, 2003b). Specifically, the following relationship between the rank of a document d among all documents in CD (denoted $rank(d, CD)$) and $\Pr(rel|d)$ is defined:

$$\Pr(rel|d) = \begin{cases} c_q, & if \quad rank(d, CD) < r * |CD| \\ 0, & \text{otherwise} \end{cases} \tag{3.4}$$

where c_q is a query dependent constant ($0.002 \leq c_q \leq 0.005$ has been experimentally shown to perform well (Si and Callan, 2003b)) and r is a threshold indicating the percentage of the documents in CD that have a chance to be relevant to q ($r = 0.003$ was used in (Si and Callan, 2003b)). Basically, Formula (3.4) states that documents from CD that are ranked among the top $r * |CD|$ have probability c_q to be relevant to q. Since $rank(d, CD)$ in Formula (3.4) is not directly available, it needs to be estimated, which can be done based on the ranks of different documents in the centralized sample document collection CSD (Si and Callan, 2003b):

$$rank(d, CD) = \sum_{d_i : rank(d_i, CSD) < rank(d, CSD)} \frac{|S_i|}{|SD(S_i)|} \tag{3.5}$$

where d_i is a document in S_i. A hidden assumption behind this formula is that each document in $SD(S_i)$ represents $|S_i|/|SD(S_i)|$ documents in S_i. Thus, for every document d_i that is ranked ahead of d in CSD, there are $|S_i|/|SD(S_i)|$ documents in CD that are ranked ahead of d in CD.

One problem with the ReDDE algorithm is that its ranking of the search engines has the effect of favoring the recall measure (it ranks search engines with more relevant documents higher) while paying little attention to the precision measure (i.e., the ranking of the relevant documents in each search engine is not considered). On the other hand, many search applications prefer results with high precision.

The UUM (*unified utility maximization framework*) algorithm (Si and Callan, 2004) can adjust the performance goal, i.e., targeting either high precision or high recall, according to the need. UUM employs a more sophisticated method to estimate the probabilities of relevance of documents in different search engines. This method uses a set of training queries and human relevance judgment for a set of retrieved documents for each training query to build a logistic model for mapping global similarities based on CD to probabilities of relevance.

When the user submits a new query q, UUM first uses the global similarities of the sample documents in CSD to estimate the global similarities of all documents in each search engine S_i using a curve-fitting technique. Specifically, the documents in $SD(S_i)$ are ranked in descending order of their global similarities, and the j-th ranked document d_j is assumed to be ranked at the k_j-th position among all the documents in S_i, where $k_j = (j/2) * |S_i|/|SD(S_i)|$ (i.e., each sample document in $SD(S_i)$ is assumed to represent $|S_i|/|SD(S_i)|$ documents in S_i and it is ranked in the middle of these documents). Linear interpolation can be applied to the points formed by the global similarities and their ranking positions of the documents in $SD(S_i)$ to generate a curve for estimating the distribution of the global similarities of all documents in S_i based on their ranks. These global similarities can then be mapped to probabilities of relevance with respect to q using the above trained logistic model.

The ability to map different local ranks to different probabilities of relevance makes it possible to adjust performance goal easily. Specifically, if the goal is to achieve high recall, UUM estimates the number of relevant documents in each search engine and ranks the search engines in descending order of this number. This is similar to the ReDDE algorithm except that UUM uses a new method to estimate the probabilities of relevance. If the goal is to achieve high precision, UUM estimates the number of relevant documents among certain top ranked documents with respect to q in each search engine and ranks the search engines based on the estimated numbers.

The CRCS (*central-rank-based collection selection*) method (Shokouhi, M., 2007) ranks search engines for a given query q based on a ranking score for each search engine that is computed based on two factors. The first is the ranking positions of the sampled documents from each search engine when q is evaluated against the centralized sample document collection *CSD*, and the second is the average number of documents in each search engine that can be represented by a sampled document from the search engine. Let $rs(S_i, q)$ denote the ranking score of S_i for q.

CRCS first evaluates q against *CSD* to obtain a ranked list (denoted as *RL*) of the documents in *CSD* based on the global similarities. Intuitively, if a document from $SD(S_i)$ is ranked higher in *RL*, it has a larger impact on determining the usefulness of S_i for q. CRCS measures this impact using the following function:

$$imp(d_j) = \begin{cases} \gamma - j, & if \quad j < \gamma \\ 0, & \text{otherwise} \end{cases} \tag{3.6}$$

where d_j is the j-th ranked document in *RL* and γ is a rank threshold indicating that only the top γ documents in *RL* are considered to have an impact (γ = 50 was used in (Shokouhi, M., 2007)). Another impact function that has been considered is (Shokouhi, M., 2007):

$$imp(d_j) = \alpha \exp(-\beta \times j) \tag{3.7}$$

where α and β are two constant parameters that were set to 1.2 and 2.8, respectively. Function (3.7) produced slightly better result than function (3.6) according to the experimental results (Shokouhi, M., 2007).

Approximately, each sample document in $SD(S_i)$ represents $|S_i|/|SD(S_i)|$ documents in S_i. As a result, a sample document from a search engine with a larger $|S|/|SD(S)|$ ratio should have a larger impact. In other words, the impact of a sample document should be weighted by the above ratio. The ratio is normalized by the size of the largest search engine (we use max S to denote this size) (Shokouhi, M., 2007).

The above discussions can be summarized as follows. When the documents in *CSD* are ranked for a given query, search engines that have more highly-ranked sample documents and whose sample documents can represent more documents in their search engines should be ranked high. Based on this summary, the following formula is used to compute the ranking score of search engine S_i with respect to query q (Shokouhi, M., 2007):

$$rs(S_i, q) = \frac{|S_i|}{\max S \times |SD(S_i)|} \sum_{d \in SD(S_i)} imp(d). \tag{3.8}$$

Finally, search engines are ranked in descending order of their ranking scores as computed by Formula (3.8).

3.4 STATISTICAL REPRESENTATIVE APPROACHES

A statistical representative of a search engine typically takes every term in every document indexed by the search engine into consideration and keeps one or more pieces of statistics for each such term. As a result, this type of representative permits more accurate estimation of the usefulness of a search engine with respect to any given query. Thus, it is not surprising that most search engine selection algorithms that have been proposed in the literature are based on statistical representatives. In this subsection, we describe five such approaches.

3.4.1 D-WISE

In the D-WISE metasearch engine (Yuwono and Lee, 1997), the representative of a search engine consists of the document frequency of each term in the document collection of the search engine and the size (i.e., number of documents) of this collection. Therefore, the representative of a search engine with n distinct terms will contain $n+1$ quantities (the document frequencies of the n terms and the size of the search engine) in addition to the n terms. In the following discussion, we use n_i to denote the number of documents indexed by the i-th search engine S_i and df_{ij} to denote the document frequency of term t_j in S_i.

In D-WISE, the representatives of all component search engines are used to compute the ranking score of each search engine with respect to a given query q. The scores measure the relative usefulness of all search engines with respect to q. If the score of search engine S_1 is higher than that of search engine S_2, then S_1 will be judged to be more relevant to q than S_2. The ranking scores are computed as follows. First, the *cue validity* of each query term, say term t_j, for search engine S_i, CV_{ij}, is computed using the following formula:

$$CV_{ij} = \frac{\frac{df_{ij}}{n_i}}{\frac{df_{ij}}{n_i} + \frac{\sum_{k \neq i}^{N} df_{kj}}{\sum_{k \neq i}^{N} n_k}} \tag{3.9}$$

where N is the number of component search engines in the metasearch engine. Intuitively, CV_{ij} measures the percentage of the documents in S_i that contain term t_j relative to that in all other search engines. If S_i has a higher percentage of documents containing t_j in comparison to the rest of the search engines, then CV_{ij} tends to have a larger value. Next, the *variance* of the CV_{ij}'s of each query term t_j for all component search engines, CVV_j, is computed as follows:

$$CVV_j = \frac{\sum_{i=1}^{N} (CV_{ij} - ACV_j)^2}{N} \tag{3.10}$$

where ACV_j is the average of all CV_{ij}'s of t_j across all component search engines. The value CVV_j can be interpreted as measuring the skew of the distribution of term t_j across all component search engines. For two terms t_u and t_v, if CVV_u is larger than CVV_v, then term t_u is more useful in differentiating different component search engines than term t_v. As an extreme case, if every search engine had the same percentage of documents containing a term, then the term would have little use for search engine selection (the *CVV* of the term would be zero in this case). Finally, the ranking score of component search engine S_i with respect to query q is computed by:

$$r_i = \sum_{j=1}^{k} CVV_j * df_{ij} \tag{3.11}$$

where k is the number of terms in the query. It can be seen that the ranking score of S_i is the sum of the document frequencies of all query terms in S_i, weighted by each query term's *CVV* (recall that the value of *CVV* for a term reflects the distinguishing power of the term). Intuitively, the ranking scores provide clues to where useful query terms are concentrated among the component search engines. If a search engine has many useful query terms, each appearing in a higher percentage of documents in the search engine than the rest of the search engines, then the ranking score of the search engine will be high. After the ranking scores of all search engines are computed with respect to a given query, the search engines with the highest scores will be selected for search for this query.

The representative of a search engine in D-WISE contains one quantity, i.e., the document frequency, per distinct term in the search engine, plus one additional quantity, the size, for the search engine. As a result, this approach is highly scalable. The computation is also simple. However, there are two problems with this approach. First, the ranking scores are relative scores. As a result, it will be difficult to determine the real usefulness of a search engine with respect to a given query. If there are no good search engines for a given query, then even the top ranked search engine will have very little value for the query. On the other hand, if there are many good search engines for another query, then even the 10th ranked search engine can still be very useful. Relative ranking scores are not very useful in differentiating these situations. Second, the accuracy of this approach is questionable as it does not differentiate the case where a document contains, say, one occurrence of a term from the case where a document contains 100 occurrences of the same term.

3.4.2 CORI NET

In the Collection Retrieval Inference Network (CORI Net) approach (Callan et al., 1995), the representative of a search engine consists of, for each distinct term, the *document frequency* of the term. In addition, the metasearch engine also contains for each distinct term, the *collection frequency*, which is the number of component search engines that contain the term.

In CORI Net, for a given query q, a document ranking technique known as *inference network* (Turtle and Croft, 1991), which is used in the INQUERY document retrieval system (Callan et al., 1992), is extended to rank all component search engines with respect to q. The extension is mostly conceptual, and the main idea is to treat the representative of a search engine as a super document and the set of all representatives as a collection of super documents. Intuitively, the representative of a search engine may be conceptually considered as a super document containing all distinct terms in the document collection of the search engine. If a term appears in k documents in the search engine, we repeat the term k times in the super document. As a result, the document frequency of a term in the search engine becomes the *term frequency* of the term in the super document. The set of all super documents of the component search engines in the metasearch engine form a collection of super documents. Let C denote this collection of all super documents. Then the original *collection frequency* of a term becomes the document frequency of the term in C. Therefore, from the representatives of component search engines, we can obtain the term frequency and document frequency of each term in each super document. In principle, the *tfw*idfw* (term frequency weight times inverse document frequency weight) formula can now be used to compute the weight of each term in each super document so as to represent each super document as a vector of terms with weights. Furthermore, a similarity function such as the *Cosine function* (Formula (1.2)) can be used to compute the similarities (ranking scores) of all super documents (i.e., search engine representatives) with respect to query q, and these similarities can then be used to rank all component search engines. The search engine ranking approach employed in CORI Net is an inference network based probabilistic approach.

In CORI Net, the ranking score of a search engine with respect to query q is an estimated belief that the search engine contains useful documents. The belief is essentially the combined probability that the search engine contains useful documents due to each query term. More specifically, the belief is computed as follows. Suppose the user query contains k terms $t_1, \ldots, t_k$. Let N be the number of component search engines in the metasearch engine. Let df_{ij} be the document frequency of the j-th term t_j in the i-th component search engine S_i and cf_j be the collection frequency of t_j. First, the belief that S_i contains useful documents due to t_j is computed by:

$$p(t_j|S_i) = c_1 + (1 - c_1) * T_{ij} * I_j \tag{3.12}$$

where

$$T_{ij} = c_2 + (1 - c_2) * \frac{df_{ij}}{df_{ij} + K} \tag{3.13}$$

is a formula for computing the term frequency weight of t_j in the super document corresponding to S_i and

$$I_j = \frac{\log\left(\frac{N+0.5}{cf_j}\right)}{\log(N + 1.0)} \tag{3.14}$$

is a formula for computing the inverse document frequency weight of t_j based on all super documents. In Formulas (3.12) and (3.13), c_1 and c_2 are constants between 0 and 1, and $K =$

$c_3 * ((1 - c_4) + c_4 * cw_i/acw)$ is a function of the number of words in S_i with c_3 and c_4 being two constants, cw_i being the number of distinct words in S_i, and *acw* being the average number of distinct words in a component search engine. The values of these constants (c_1, c_2, c_3 and c_4) can be determined empirically by performing experiments on test collections. Note that the value of $p(t_j|S_i)$ is essentially the *tfw*idfw* weight of term t_j in the super document corresponding to search engine S_i. Next, the significance of term t_j in representing query q, denoted $p(q|t_j)$, can be estimated, for example, to be the query term weight of t_j in q. Finally, the belief that S_i contains useful documents with respect to query q, or the ranking score of S_i with respect to q, can be estimated by

$$r_i = p(q|S_i) = \sum_{j=1}^{k} p(q|t_j) * p(t_j|S_i). \tag{3.15}$$

In CORI Net, the representative of a search engine contains slightly more than one piece of information per term, i.e., the *document frequency* plus the shared *collection frequency* across all component search engines). Therefore, the CORI Net approach also has rather good scalability. The information for representing each component search engine can also be obtained and maintained easily. An advantage of the CORI Net approach is that the same method can be used to compute the ranking score of a document with a query as well as the ranking score of a search engine (through the search engine representative or super document) with a query. It has been shown (Xu and Callan, 1998) that if phrase information is collected and stored in each search engine representative, and queries are expanded based on a technique called *local context analysis* (Xu and Croft, 1996), then the CORI Net approach can select useful search engines more accurately.

3.4.3 GGLOSS

In the gGlOSS (generalized Glossary Of Servers' Server) system (Gravano and Garcia-Molina, 1995), each component search engine is represented by a set of pairs (df_i, W_i), where df_i is the document frequency of the i-th term t_i and W_i is the sum of the weights of t_i over all documents in the component search engine. A threshold T is associated with each query in gGlOSS to indicate that the user is only interested in documents whose similarities with the query are higher than T. Specifically, in gGlOSS, the usefulness of a search engine S with respect to a query q and a similarity threshold T is defined as follows:

$$usefulness(S, q, T) = \sum_{d \in S \cap sim(d,q) > T} sim(d, q) \tag{3.16}$$

where $sim(d, q)$ denote the similarity between a document d and query q. The usefulness of each component search engine is used as the ranking score of the search engine.

We now need to estimate the usefulness of any given component search engine as defined by Formula (3.16). It turns out that making the estimation directly is difficult. In gGlOSS, two methods are proposed to estimate the usefulness based on following two assumptions:

- *High-correlation assumption*: For any given component search engine, if query term t_i appears in at least as many documents as query term t_j, then every document containing term t_j also contains term t_i.

- *Disjointness assumption*: For any given component search engine, for any two query terms t_i and t_j, the set of documents containing t_i is disjoint from the set of documents containing t_j.

It is not difficult to see that the above two assumptions are unlikely to hold in practice. As a result, the estimated search engine usefulness based on these assumptions will be inaccurate. On the other hand, of the two estimation methods proposed in gGlOSS, the one based on the high-correlation assumption tends to overestimate the usefulness and the one based on the disjointness assumption tends to underestimate the usefulness. Since the two estimates by the two formulas tend to form upper and lower bounds of the true usefulness, the two methods are more useful when used together than when used separately.

We now discuss the two estimation methods for a search engine S. Suppose $q = (q_1, \ldots, q_k)$ is the query under consideration and T is the associated threshold, where q_i is the weight of term t_i in q. It is further assumed that the similarity function *sim*( ) is the dot-product function.

High-correlation case: Let query terms be arranged in ascending order of document frequency, i.e., $df_i \leq df_j$ for any $i < j$. Based on the high-correlation assumption, every document containing t_i also contains t_j for any $j > i$. Thus, there are df_1 documents each having similarity $\sum_{i=1}^{k} q_i * \frac{W_i}{df_i}$ with q. In general, there are $df_j - df_{j-1}$ documents each having similarity $\sum_{i=j}^{k} q_i * \frac{W_i}{df_i}$ with q, $1 \leq j \leq k$ and df_0 is defined to be 0. Let p be an integer between 1 and k that satisfies $\sum_{i=p}^{k} q_i * \frac{W_i}{df_i} > T$ and $\sum_{i=p+1}^{k} q_i * \frac{W_i}{df_i} \leq T$. Then the estimated usefulness of this search engine is:

$$\begin{aligned} usefulness(S, q, T) &= \sum_{j=1}^{p} (df_j - df_{j-1}) * \left(\sum_{i=j}^{k} q_i * \frac{W_i}{df_i} \right) \\ &= \sum_{j=1}^{p} q_j * W_j + df_p * \sum_{j=p+1}^{k} q_j * \frac{W_j}{df_j}. \end{aligned} \tag{3.17}$$

Disjointness case: By the disjointness assumption, each document can contain at most one query term. Thus, there are df_i documents that contain term t_i and the similarity of each of these df_i documents with query q is $q_i * W_i / df_i$. Therefore, the estimated usefulness of component search engine S in the disjoint case is:

$$
\begin{aligned}
usefulness(S, q, T) &= \sum_{i=1,\ldots,k|df_i>0 \cap q_i * \frac{W_i}{df_i} > T} df_i * q_i * \frac{W_i}{df_i} \\
&= \sum_{i=1,\ldots,k|df_i>T \cap q_i * \frac{W_i}{df_i} > T} q_i * W_i . \qquad (3.18)
\end{aligned}
$$

In gGlOSS, the usefulness of a search engine is sensitive to the similarity threshold used. As a result, gGlOSS can differentiate a search engine with many moderately similar documents from a search engine with a few highly similar documents by choosing a suitable threshold T. This is not possible in D-WISE and CORI Net. For a given search engine, the size of the search engine representative in gGlOSS is twice the size of that in D-WISE. The computation for estimating the search engine usefulness in gGlOSS is fairly simple and can be carried out efficiently.

3.4.4 NUMBER OF POTENTIALLY USEFUL DOCUMENTS

An interesting search engine usefulness measure is the number of potentially useful documents with respect to a given query in a search engine. This measure can be useful for search services that charge a fee for each search. If the fee is independent of the number of retrieved documents, then from the user's perspective, a component search engine that contains a large number of similar documents but not necessarily the most similar documents is preferable to another component system containing just a few most similar documents. On the other hand, if a fee is charged for each retrieved document, then the component search engine having a few of the most similar documents would be preferred. This type of charging policy can be incorporated into the search engine selector of a metasearch engine if the number of potentially useful documents in a search engine with respect to a given query can be estimated.

Let S be a component search engine and $sim(q,d)$ be the *global similarity* between a query q and a document d in S. Here the global similarity is computed using a global similarity function defined in the metasearch engine based on appropriate global term statistics. For example, if document frequency of a term is used, it will be the global document frequency of the term, i.e., the total number of documents that contain the term in all component search engines. Let T be a similarity threshold used to define what a potentially useful document is. That is, any document whose similarity with q is higher than T is considered to be potentially useful. Now the number of potentially useful documents in S, with respect to q, can be precisely defined as follows:

$$NoDoc(S, q, T) = |\{d | d \in S \cap sim(d, q) > T\}| \qquad (3.19)$$

where $|X|$ denotes the size of the set X.

If $NoDoc(S, q, T)$ can be accurately estimated, then the search engine selector can simply select those search engines with the most potentially useful documents to search for query q.

A generating-function based method has been proposed to estimate $NoDoc(S, q, T)$ when the global similarity function is the *dot product function* (the widely used *Cosine function* is a special case of the *dot product function* with normalized term weights) (Meng et al., 1998). In this method, the representative of a search engine with n distinct terms consists of n pairs $\{(p_i, w_i)\}$, i= 1, ..., n, where p_i is the probability that term t_i appears in a document in S (note that p_i is simply the document frequency of term t_i in S divided by the number of documents in S) and w_i is the average of the weights of t_i in the set of documents containing t_i. Let $(q_1, q_2, ..., q_k)$ be the query vector of query q, where q_i is the weight of query term t_i. Here, q_i incorporates the global inverse document frequency as well as the term frequency of t_i.

Consider the following generating function:

$$\prod_{i=1}^{k} \left(p_i * X^{w_i * q_i} + (1 - p_i)\right). \tag{3.20}$$

After the generating function (3.20) is expanded and the coefficients of terms with the same X^s are combined, we obtain

$$\sum_{i=1}^{c} a_i * X^{b_i}, \quad b_1 > b_2 > \cdots > b_c. \tag{3.21}$$

It can be shown that, if the terms are independent and the weight of term t_i whenever present in a document is w_i, which is given in the search engine representative ($1 \leq i \leq k$), then a_i is the probability that a document in S has similarity b_i with q (Meng et al., 1998). Therefore, if S has n documents, then $n * a_i$ is the expected number of documents in S that have similarity b_i with query q. For a given similarity threshold T, let C be the largest integer to satisfy $b_C > T$. Then $NoDoc(S, q, T)$ can be estimated by the following formula:

$$NoDoc(S, q, T) = \sum_{i=1}^{C} n * a_i = n \sum_{i=1}^{C} a_i. \tag{3.22}$$

The above solution has two restrictive assumptions. The first is the *term independence assumption* and the second is the *uniform term weight assumption*, i.e., the weights of a term in all documents containing the term are the same – the average weight). These assumptions reduce the accuracy of the estimation of $NoDoc(S, q, T)$ in practice. One way to address the term independence assumption is to utilize *covariances* between term pairs, term triplets, and so on and to incorporate them into the generating-function (3.20) (Meng et al., 1998). The problem with this method is that the storage overhead for representing a component search engine will become too large because of the huge number of covariances. A remedy is to use only significant covariances, i.e., those whose absolute values are significantly greater than zero. Another way to incorporate dependencies between terms is to combine certain adjacent terms into a single term (Liu et al., 2002a). This is similar to recognizing phrases.

A method known as the *subrange-based estimation method* has been proposed to deal with the uniform term weight assumption (Meng et al., 1999a). This method partitions the actual weights of a term t_i in the set of documents having the term into a number of disjoint subranges of possibly different lengths. For each subrange, the median of the weights in the subrange is estimated based on the assumption that the weight distribution of the term is *normal*. The estimation requires that the standard deviation of the weights of the term be added to the search engine representative. Then, the weights of t_i that fall in a given subrange are approximated by the median of the weights in the subrange. With this weight approximation, for a query containing term t_i, the polynomial $p_i * X^{w_i * q_i} + (1 - p_i)$ in the generating function (3.20) is replaced by the following polynomial:

$$p_{i1} * X^{wm_{i1} * q_i} + p_{i2} * X^{wm_{i2} * q_i} + \cdots + p_{ir} * X^{wm_{ir} * q_i} + (1 - p_i)$$

where p_{ij} is the probability that term t_i appears in a document in search engine S and has a weight in the j-th subrange, wm_{ij} is the median of the weights of t_i in the j-th subrange, $j = 1, \ldots, r$, and r is the number of subranges used. After the new generating function is obtained, the rest of the estimation process is identical to that described earlier. It was shown that if the *maximum normalized weight* of each term, which is the maximum of the normalized weights of the term in all documents of S, is used as a subrange (i.e., the highest subrange) by itself, the estimation accuracy of the search engine usefulness can be drastically improved (Meng et al., 1999b).

The above methods, while being able to produce accurate estimation, have a large storage overhead. Furthermore, the computation complexity of expanding the generating function is exponential. As a result, they are more suitable for short queries.

3.4.5 SIMILARITY OF THE MOST SIMILAR DOCUMENT

Another useful measure is the global similarity of the most similar document in a search engine with respect to a given query. On the one hand, this measure indicates the best that we can expect from a search engine as no other documents in the search engine can have higher similarities with the query. On the other hand, for a given query, this measure can be used to rank search engines optimally for retrieving the m most similar documents across all search engines for any given positive integer m.

Suppose a user wants the metasearch engine to find the m most similar documents to his/her query q across N component search engines $S_1, S_2, \ldots, S_N$ based on a global similarity function. The following definition defines an optimal order of these search engines for the query.

Definition 3.2 *A set of N search engines is said to be optimally ranked in the order [$S_1, S_2, \ldots, S_N$] with respect to query q if, for any m, there exists a k such that $S_1, S_2, \ldots, S_k$ contain the m most similar documents and each S_i, $1 \leq i \leq k$, contains at least one of the m most similar documents.*

Intuitively, the order given in Definition 3.2 is optimal because the m desired documents to the query, no matter what m is, are always contained in the first k search engines for some k and each of these k search engines contributes at least one of the desired documents.

The proposition below gives a necessary and sufficient condition for the search engines S_1, S_2, ..., S_N to be optimally ranked with respect to query q (Yu et al., 2002). For simplicity, this proposition assumes that all documents have different similarities with the query so that the set of the m most similar documents to the query is unique.

Proposition 3.3 *Search engines [S_1, S_2, ..., S_N] are optimally ranked with respect to a query q if and only if they are ranked in descending order of the similarity of the most similar document in each search engine.*

Note that the above necessary and sufficient condition is independent of the similarity function used to compute the global similarities. In fact, if there is a relevance function that assigns degrees of relevance to documents, the same result will also be applicable. Thus, this condition can be applied to all types of search engines, including image, audio, and video search engines.

Let $msim(S, q)$ denote the similarity of the most similar document in S with respect to q based on a global similarity function employed by the metasearch engine. Proposition 3.3 says that if the search engines are ranked in the order such that $msim(S_1, q) > msim(S_2, q) > \ldots > msim(S_N, q)$, then $[S_1, S_2, ..., S_N]$ is an optimal order for q. Knowing an optimal rank of the search engines with respect to query q, the search engine selector can select the top-ranked search engines to search for q. Note that if not all similarities of the documents with the query are distinct, Proposition 3.3 remains essentially true (need to change "in descending order" to "in non-ascending order" in the proposition), but the optimal order may no longer be unique. In this case, for any positive integer m, there is a k, such that the top k search engines contain one set of m documents that have the highest similarities with q among all documents, and each of these search engines contains at least one document in the set.

To apply Proposition 3.3 in practice, we need to know $msim(S, q)$ for each component search engine S with respect to any query q. We now discuss how to estimate $msim(S, q)$ for any query q and any search engine S using certain search engine representative for S. One method is to utilize the Expression (3.21) for S. We can scan this expression in descending order of the exponents until $\sum_{i=1}^{r} a_i * n$ is approximately 1 for some r, where n is the number of documents in S. Then the exponent, b_r, is an estimate of $msim(S, q)$ as the expected number of documents in S with similarity greater than or equal to b_r is approximately 1. The drawback of this solution is that it requires a large search engine representative and the computation is of exponential complexity in the number of terms in the query.

We now introduce a more efficient method to estimate $msim(S, q)$ (Yu et al., 2002). In this method, there are two types of representatives. There is a global representative for all component search engines. For each distinct term t_i, the global inverse document frequency weight ($gidf_i$) is stored in this representative. There is a local representative for each component search engine S. For each distinct term t_i in S, a pair of quantities (mnw_i, anw_i) is stored, where mnw_i and anw_i are the *maximum normalized weight* and the *average normalized weight* of term t_i, respectively. Suppose d_i is the weight of t_i in a document d. Then the normalized weight of t_i in d is $d_i/|d|$, where $|d|$

denotes the length of d. The *maximum normalized weight* and the *average normalized weight* of t_i in search engine S are, respectively, the maximum and the average of the normalized weights of t_i in all documents in S. Suppose $q = (q_1, \ldots, q_k)$ is the query vector. Then $msim(S, q)$ can be estimated as follows:

$$msim(S,q) = \max_{1 \le i \le k} \left\{ q_i * gidf_i * mnw_i + \sum_{1 \le j \le k, j \ne i} q_j * gidf_j * anw_j \right\} \Big/ |q|. \tag{3.23}$$

The intuition behind this estimation formula is as follows. The most similar document in a search engine is likely to have the maximum normalized weight on one of the query terms, say t_i. This yields the first half of the above expression within the braces. For each of the remaining query terms, the document takes the average normalized weight. This is represented by the second half of the above expression. The maximum is taken over all query terms because the most similar document may have the maximum normalized weight on any one of the k query terms. Normalization by the query length, defined as $|q| = \sqrt{q_1^2 + \ldots + q_k^2}$, yields a value less than or equal to 1. The underlying assumption of Formula (3.23) is that terms in each query are independent. Dependencies between terms can be captured to certain extent by storing the same statistics, i.e., *mnw*'s and *anw*'s) of phrases in the search engine representatives, i.e., treating each phrase as a term.

In this method, each search engine is represented by two quantities per term plus the global representative shared by all search engines. It is easy to see that the estimation, using Formula (3.23), has linear complexity in the number of query terms.

The maximum normalized weight of a term is typically two or more orders of magnitude larger than the average normalized weight of the term (Wu et al., 2001). The reason is that the average normalized weight of a term is computed over all documents, including those that do not contain the term. This observation implies that in Formula (3.23), if all query terms have the same *tf* weight, which is a reasonable assumption, since in a typical query each term appears once, then $gidf_i * mnw_i$ is likely to dominate $\sum_{j=1, j \ne i}^{k} gidf_j * anw_j$, especially when the number of terms, k, in a query is small, which is typically true in the Internet environment. In other words, the rank of search engine S with respect to a given query q is largely determined by the value of $\max_{1 \le i \le k} \{q_i * gidf_i * mnw_i\}$. This leads to the following more scalable formula to estimate $msim(S, q)$ (Wu et al., 2001):

$$msim(S,q) = \max_{1 \le i \le k} \{q_i * am_i\}, \tag{3.24}$$

where $am_i = gidf_i * mnw_i$ is called the *adjusted maximum normalized weight* of term t_i in S. This formula requires only one piece of information, namely am_i, to be kept in the search engine representative for each distinct term in the search engine.

For a truly large-scale metasearch engine with hundreds of thousands of component search engines, keeping a separate search engine representative for each component search engine may not be practical in terms of both computation efficiency and storage efficiency. Specifically, not only hundreds of thousands of search engine representatives need to be stored, the same number of similarities of the most similar documents in these search engines need to be estimated for each query. One scheme that can overcome these inefficiencies is to integrate the representatives of all component search engines into a single, integrated representative (Meng et al., 2001). Let $am(t, S)$ denote the adjusted maximum normalized weight of term t in search engine S. For each term t, among the *am*'s from all component search engines, the integrated representative keeps only the r largest ones for a small integer r (say ≤ 50) and discards the rest. The idea is that if a component search engine does not have one of the r largest weights for t, then it is unlikely to be among the most useful search engines for a query containing t. If $am(t, S)$ is kept in the integrated representative for t, then the id# of search engine S is kept as well. In other words, up to r pairs $(am(t, S_i), \text{id\#}(S_i))$ are kept for t in the integrated representative.

Based on the integrated representative, the following efficient search engine ranking process can be employed: For query q, first identify the r pairs $(am(t, S_i), \text{id\#}(S_i))$ for each term t in q; then we estimate the similarity of the most similar document for each search engine whose id# is in these pairs using Formula (3.24); finally rank the search engines in descending order of these quantities. Clearly, if q has k distinct terms, then at most $r * k$ similarity estimations need to be performed, independent of the number of component search engines in the metasearch engine. For a typical Internet query with 2–3 terms and for $r = 50$, only 100–150 simple computations are needed to rank all the component search engines approximately optimally. As a result, this method is highly scalable in terms of computation.

The above integrated representative can also scale to a virtually unlimited number of search engines in terms of its size. Suppose there is a rough bound on the number of distinct terms, say $M = 10$ million, regardless of the number of component search engines in the metasearch engine. For each term, the integrated representative stores $2 * r$ quantities (the r largest adjusted maximum normalized weights and r search engine identifiers). Therefore, the total size of this representative is bounded by $(10 + 4 * 2 * r) * M$ bytes, assuming that each term occupies 10 bytes on the average and each quantity occupies 4 bytes. When $r = 50$ and $M = 10$ million, $(10 + 4 * 2 * r) * M = 4.1$ GB, which can easily be accommodated by the memory capacity of a reasonable server. The good scalability of the integrated representative approach is due to the fact that it stores only a small constant number of quantities for each term regardless of how many search engines may contain the term.

The search engine selection algorithm based on the integrated representative is used by the AllInOneNews metasearch engine (`http://www.allinonenews.com/`) (Liu et al., 2007).

3.4.6 SEARCH ENGINE REPRESENTATIVE GENERATION

One critical issue related to statistical representative approaches is how to obtain the statistics related to each term. Without these statistics, we will not be able to implement the search engine selection algorithms introduced above. Below, we consider several different scenarios and discuss how to obtain the desired term statistics for each scenario.

1. *Component search engines are fully cooperative.* While most metasearch engines are built on top of autonomous search engines, it is possible that a metasearch engine includes only cooperative search engines. In this case, the metasearch engine can require each participating search engine to provide the desired term statistics about its own documents. In fact, in this scenario, the metasearch engine may provide appropriate tools to participating search engines for them to collect the desired statistics uniformly.

2. *Component search engines' contents are independently obtainable.* For example, a metasearch engine could be created to support unified access to the search engines of the 64 campuses of the State University of New York System. The searchable content of the search engine for each campus is the set of Web pages at the campus' Web site. These Web pages are easily crawlable starting from the campus homepage. In this scenario, the Web pages of each campus can be crawled and used to compute the search engine representative for the campus.

3. *Component search engines follow a certain protocol for providing term statistics.* As discussed in Section 2.3.2, a number of protocols have been proposed in the search and metasearch community to make the interactions between search engines and metasearch engines easier. Some of these protocols, noticeably STARTS (Gravano et al., 1997), specifically require search engines to return certain statistics for terms that are submitted as queries. There are two problems with the currently proposed protocols. First, not all the statistics needed by different search engine selection techniques are required to be returned. Second, none of these protocols is widely adopted by current search engines.

4. *Component search engines are uncooperative and their contents are not crawlable.* For such a search engine, it will be difficult to accurately obtain the term statistics needed by the search engine representative. A general solution proposed in literature is to generate an approximate search engine representative using a set of sampled documents retrieved from the search engine. This solution can be conceptually considered as consisting of two steps. In the first step, an approximate vocabulary for each search engine is obtained, which captures the important terms of the document collection of the search engine. Important terms are content terms that have high occurrences in the search engine's document collection. This step also generates a set of sample documents (the approximate vocabulary contains terms from this sample set) and this sample set itself is useful for sample documents based search engine selection techniques (see Section 3.3). In the second step, the desired statistics of each term in the obtained vocabulary are obtained. These two steps are further discussed below.

   To obtain an approximate vocabulary of a search engine, a query-based sampling technique can be used to produce sample documents from which terms of the vocabulary are identified (Callan et al., 1999). This approach works as follows. First, select a term as an initial query and submit it to the search engine. Next, select new terms from some top ranked documents returned by the search engine and submit each selected term as a query to the search engine.

Repeat this process until a stopping condition is satisfied. The selected terms form an approximate vocabulary of the search engine. One proposed metric to measure the quality of the vocabulary is the *ctf ratio*, where *ctf* represents *collection term frequency* – the total number of occurrences a term appears in a document collection (Callan et al., 1999). This metric is the total *ctf*s of the content terms in the approximate vocabulary, divided by the total *ctf*s of the content words in the search engine's document collection.

The experiments show that (1) selecting the initial query term and subsequent query terms randomly has little effect on the final quality of the learned vocabulary in terms of covering the total number of occurrences of the terms in the search engine's document collection, (2) it is sufficient to examine a small number of top ranked documents for each query (top 4 were used in the above work but smaller numbers also worked reasonably well), and (3) examining a small number of documents (around 300) can yield a *ctf* ratio above 80% (Callan et al., 1999).

An improved process for generating an approximate vocabulary of a search engine's document collection is to use pre-generated probe queries associated with different categories in a category hierarchy to determine the right category or categories of each component search engine S (Ipeirotis and Gravano, 2002). This is carried out in a top-down fashion, that is, only when a higher-level category C is determined to be sufficiently relevant to S, the child categories of C will be explored (i.e., only the probe queries related to these child categories will be submitted to S) to see if they are appropriate for S. Here whether a category C is sufficiently relevant to S is determined based on two quantities denoted as *Coverage*(C) and *Specificity*(C), where the former is the number of documents in S belonging to C, and the latter is the fraction of documents in S that belong to C. Both quantities are estimated based on the numbers of results retrieved when probe queries associated with different categories are submitted to S. Category C is sufficiently relevant to S if both *Coverage*(C) and *Specificity*(C) exceed certain pre-specified thresholds. This top-down categorization process allows more relevant queries to be submitted to S. As a result, the sample documents, retrieved from S using these queries, tend to be more representative of the contents of S's document collection than those by random queries. For each probe query submitted to S, only a small number of top-ranked documents are placed into the sample document set for S. Content terms that appear in the sample documents retrieved from S form the approximate vocabulary for S's document collection. Experimental results (Ipeirotis and Gravano, 2002) confirm that the quality (i.e., *ctf ratio*) of the vocabularies, produced by the improved method, is significantly better than that by the method proposed by Callan et al. (1999).

Once the approximate vocabulary V for a search engine S is obtained, desired statistics for each term t in V can be estimated in a number of ways. One of the most popular statistics used by different search engine selection algorithms is *document frequency* (*df*). A simple way to obtain a good approximation of the *df* for t is to submit t to S and let the number of documents retrieved be the *df*. Most search engines return this number and therefore no actual documents need to be retrieved. We should note that the size of V is typically a small fraction of that of the complete vocabulary of a search engine even though V can achieve good *ctf ratio* (Callan et al., 1999).

A method for estimating the *dfs* of all terms in V without submitting each t as a query exists (Ipeirotis and Gravano, 2002). During the generation of V, the *dfs* of the terms in V among the sampled documents are computed and the actual *dfs* of some terms used in single-term probe queries are recorded. The former *dfs* are used to rank the terms in the sampled document in descending *df* values. For terms with actual *dfs*, their *dfs* and their ranks are then used to estimate the parameters in the Mandelbrot formula (Mandelbrot, B., 1988), $df = P * (r + p)^{-B}$, which captures the relationship between the rank r and the *df* of a term t in a document collection, where P, B, and p are parameters of the specific document collection to be estimated. Once these parameters are obtained, the actual *df* of any term t in V can be estimated by plugging in t's rank among all terms in V based on their *dfs* in the sampled documents into the above formula.

It is also possible to estimate other statistics of a term by submitting the term to a search engine. It was shown that the maximum normalized weight of a term t among all documents in a document collection based on a global term weighting formula can be quite accurately estimated from the top 20-30 ranked documents retrieved by submitting t as a query (Liu et al., 2002b).

Generating representatives from uncooperative search engines is an important issue in search engine selection and it has received a lot of attention in recent years. Shokouhi and Si (2011) have provided additional discussion on this issue.

CHAPTER 4

Search Engine Incorporation

As briefly discussed in Chapter 3, to add a component search engine to a metasearch engine, two basic programs are needed. The first is a *connector* that establishes the connection between the search engine and the metasearch engine, allowing user queries submitted to the metasearch engine interface to be sent to the server of the search engine and results retrieved from the search engine to be sent to the metasearch engine. The second is a *result extractor* that extracts the search result records on the HTML pages returned from the search engine for later use by the *result merger*. In this chapter, we discuss issues related to the implementation of search engine connectors and result extractors.

4.1 SEARCH ENGINE CONNECTION

When a user uses a search engine to perform a search, the user enters a query in the input field on the search interface and clicks on the submit button. If nothing goes wrong, the query will be forwarded to the server of the search engine, which will perform a search based on its index and returns a certain number of top ranked *search result records* (SRRs) on a dynamically generated HTML response page. In the end, the response page will be displayed to the user on the browser used.

To construct a connector for a search engine, it is necessary to have a close examination of the underlying mechanism that sends the user's query from the user's browser to the server of the search engine and sends the response page back from the search engine server to the user's browser. In this section, we first provide a brief introduction to the HTML form tag, which is commonly used to create search engine interface, and discuss how a Web browser communicates with a search engine server for query submission and result generation. Then we discuss how to automatically generate connectors for search engines.

4.1.1 HTML FORM TAG FOR SEARCH ENGINES

The Web page that contains the search interface of a search engine is usually an HTML document, and the search interface itself is programmed using the HTML *form tag* (i.e., < form > ... </form >), which is used to create HTML forms for accepting input from users. A typical HTML form of a search engine consists of an input control of *text* type, i.e., a text input control (e.g., < input type="text" name="name_string" />, where the *name* attribute specifies the name of the input, and the search engine server uses it to identify the query string), which creates the text input field, an *action* attribute (e.g., action="action_URL"), that specifies the name and location of the search engine server to which the user query will be sent when the form is submitted, a *method* attribute (e.g., method="get"), which specifies the HTTP request method for sending the query to the search engine server, and a submit input control, i.e., an input control of *submit* type (e.g., < input type="submit" value="SEARCH") that defines the name (it is "SEARCH" here) of the submit button. Other attributes and tags may also be included in a search form to specify additional features such as default settings, text styles, and the maximum length of the input text allowed. More complex search interfaces may include multiple user input controls in various formats in addition to text input fields such as selection lists, checkboxes, and radio buttons. A good source for more complete discussion of the HTML form tag can be found at the W3 Web site (`http://www.w3.org/TR/html401/interact/forms.html`[9]). Fig. 4.1 shows some of the key input controls and attributes of the form tag of the AOL search engine available at `http://www.aol.com/`.

```
<form action="http://search.aol.com/aol/search"
method="get"> <input type="hidden" name="s_it"
value="comsearch40bt1" /> <input type="text"
name="query" maxlength="150" /> <input
type="submit" value="SEARCH" /> </form>
```

Figure 4.1: An Abbreviated Form of the AOL Search Engine.[10]

From Fig. 4.1, it can be seen that the server of the AOL search engine is located at `http://search.aol.com/aol/search`, the name of the server is *search* (the string at the end of the location URL), and the HTTP request method it supports is *get*. In general, a search engine may support one of two HTTP request methods, with the other one being *post*. The *get* method permits only the retrieval of information from a remote server, and it has a limit on the size of the user input (the exact limit is browser dependent), a limit on the characters that can be used (usually only ASCII characters are permitted; non-ASCII characters can be sent only after proper encoding) and is not secure for transmitting important data over the Internet (this method should not be used to transmit userid and password). In contrast, the *post* method may request storing and updating data in addition to retrieving information. Besides, it has no limit on the size of the input data or the type of characters. The *get* method is more widely supported than the *post* method by search engines because user queries are usually short, their security requirement is low, and they require only the retrieval of information. Another benefit of the *get* method is that query response pages returned by search engines supporting the *get* method are bookmarkable, making it easier to share the response pages among different users.

With the *get* method, the user query can be submitted to the search engine server by simply appending the user query as well as other default input controls (e.g., hidden input controls) to

[9] Accessed on November 3, 2010.
[10] Obtained on December 31, 2009.

the server URL to form a new URL and submitting the new URL through the browser. More specifically, the new URL consists of the search engine server URL from the *action* attribute, a question mark symbol (?), each input in the form tag, including the user query and default input, in the form of "name=value" with the inputs being separated by the ampersand symbol (&). Non-ASCII characters, if any, need to be properly encoded (e.g., the Chinese characters 中文 are encoded as %D6%D0%CE%C4 in gbk encoding). Furthermore, if a user query has multiple terms, they are connected by the plus sign (+). As an example, when the form in Fig. 4.1 with user query "metasearch engine" is submitted, the following new URL will be generated:

```
http://search.aol.com/aol/search?s_it=comsearch
40bt1&query=metasearch+engine
```

where "s_it=comsearch" is from the hidden (default) input in Fig. 4.1. With the new URL formed, the Web browser first uses ? to divide the URL into two parts, then acts as an HTTP client agent (called user-agent) to initiate a network connection to the search engine server (its location is specified by the part before ?) and sends an HTTP *get* request message to the server with the part after ? as argument. For the above example, the server is located at search.aol.com/aol/search and the argument to the *get* request message is "s_it=comsearch40bt1&query=metasearch+engine." The following shows the format of this *get* request message sent from an IE browser version 7.0:

```
GET /aol/search?s_it=comsearch40bt1&query=
     metasearch+engine HTTP/1.1
Host: search.aol.com
User-Agent: IE/7.0
```

Once the server receives the request message, it processes the query, generates the HTML response page, and sends back an HTTP response message with the response page as the message body. Upon receiving the response page from the server, the Web browser displays it to the user.

Note that the new URL is usually viewable in the *location area* of the browser when the response page is displayed (see the URL at the top of Fig. 4.2). Now it is clear why the *get* method should not be used to transmit secure information such as userid and password.

While the *get* method is more widely used, the *post* method is also used by some search engines for various reasons such as to accommodate longer user queries and non-ASCII characters. With the *post* method, the form input data will not be encoded into a URL. Instead, the form input data will appear in the message body with appropriately specified content-length and content-type. If in the above example, the *get* method is replaced by the *post* method, then the following will be the format of *post* request message:

```
POST /aol/search HTTP/1.1
Host: search.aol.com
User-Agent: IE/7.0
Content-Length: 43
```

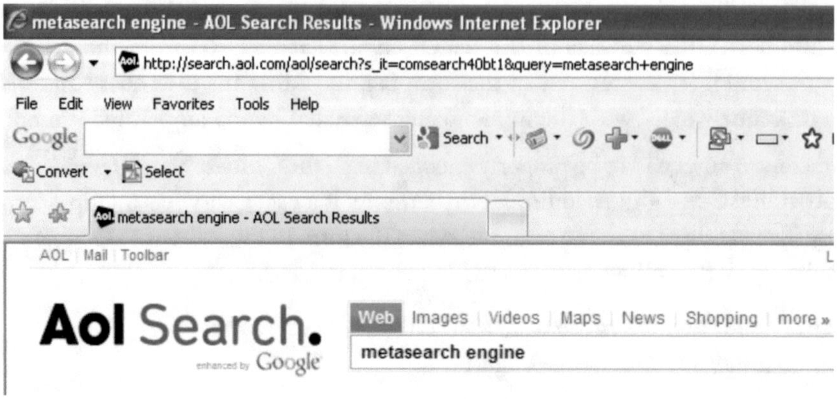

Figure 4.2: A Query URL Generated by the "get" Method.

```
Content-Type: application/x-www-form-urlencoded
s_it=comsearch40bt1&query=metasearch+engine
```

The content-type "application/x-www-form-urlencoded" indicates that the content is in the format of name-value pairs. This content type is the default when the *get* request message is generated, but it must be specified when the message content of a *post* request message consists of name-value pairs because the *post* method may be used to send other types of content.

While HTML form is most commonly used for search engine query interface implementation, there are situations where query interfaces are not built using typical HTML form. For example, the query interface on `http://www.sap.com/index.epx`[11] is implemented in flash.

4.1.2 AUTOMATIC SEARCH ENGINE CONNECTION

When a user submits a query to a search engine through a Web browser, the browser acts as the HTTP user agent for connecting to the search engine server and transmitting the request message. When a user submits a query to a metasearch engine through a Web browser, the browser also acts as the HTTP user agent for connecting to the metasearch engine server and transmitting the request message. Once the metasearch engine server receives the request message, it will extract the user query and generate an appropriate HTTP request message for each selected component search engine. Since the metasearch engine usually cannot utilize a browser to transmit the HTTP request message and receive the HTTP response message, it needs to implement its own connector to perform these tasks for each component search engine. In this subsection, we discuss how to generate a connector for a typical search engine.

[11] Accessed on September 10, 2010.

Let S be the component search engine under consideration and qs be the query string that needs to be sent to S. To generate the connector for S, three types of information about S are needed, and they are listed in Table 4.1.

Table 4.1: Information Needed for Search Engine Connection.

(1) The name and location of the search engine server.
(2) The HTTP request method (*get* or *post*) supported.
(3) The name of each input control in the search form (except the *submit* type) and its value if exists.

Fortunately, in most cases, the above information are all available in the search form of S. For example, for the AOL search engine (its search form is shown in Fig. 4.1), the name and location of its server are "search" and "search.aol.com/aol/search," respectively; its HTTP request method is "get;" it has two input controls (other than the *submit* type), the name of the *hidden* type is "s_it" and its value is "comsearch40bt1," and the name of *text* type is "query."

One requirement for automating the construction of the connector for S is the ability to automatically extract the above information from the HTML page P that contains the search interface of S. The extraction process consists of two steps. The first step is to identify the correct search form and the second step is to extract the desired information from the identified search form. We discuss these two steps below.

1. *Search form identification.* If the search form is the only HTML form on P, then this step is trivial as all we need to do is to find the form tag < form ...> ... </form >. In general, there may be multiple HTTP forms on P, and some of them may not be search forms. Example of non-search forms include forms that are used for conducting a survey, sending an email, and Web account log-in (e.g., Web-based email account or bank account). Therefore, we first need a way to differentiate search forms from non-search forms automatically. One solution (Wu et al., 2003) classifies a form as a search form if the following two conditions are satisfied: (a) The form has a text input field and (b) at least one of a set of keywords such as "search," "query" or "find" appears, either in the form tag or in the text immediately preceding or following the form tag. In another solution (Cope et al., 2003), a decision tree classifier is derived from a set of pre-classified forms using a number of automatically generated features. The decision tree obtained is shown in Fig. 4.3. In the figure, N and Y means No and Yes, respectively, and they indicate where the decision process will go next from the current node in the decision tree; SF and NSF represent search form and non-search form, respectively. The decision tree is applied in a top-down fashion to determine whether an input form is a search engine. Starting from the root of the decision tree, if the value of the submit control element of the form is "search," then the form is determined to be a search form; if the value is not "search," the classifier checks to see whether or not there is a password control element

in the form, and if the answer is yes, the form is not a search form, and if the answer is no, the classifier further checks whether word "search" is in the action string, and so on. According to the experimental results reported, the accuracy of the first method is above 90% and that of the second method is between 85% and 87%. However, different datasets are used in these experiments.

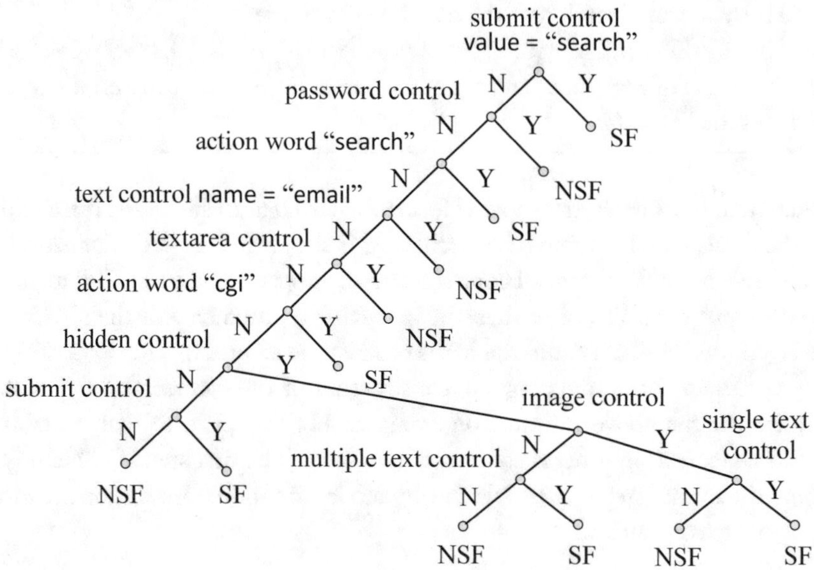

Figure 4.3: Decision Tree of Search Form Classifier (Based on (Cope et al., 2003)).

Sometimes, multiple search forms may exist on the same interface page. For example, the search interface of the Excite search engine (`http://www.excite.com/`) has 5 search forms[12]; two are identical (the main search form) but are placed at different locations (one near the top and one near the bottom), one for searching stock price, one for searching local weather, and one for searching horoscope. It is not difficult to determine the main search form on a search interface page as it is usually the first search form and is more prominently displayed (centrally located horizontally) on the interface page. However, it is possible that a user is interested in a different search engine other than the main one. In general, it is impossible to guess which search form a user might be interested to use in a metasearch engine. In this case, a reasonable solution is to let the user make the selection. This strategy is adopted by the MySearchView metasearch engine generation tool (`http://www.mysearchview.com/`). Specifically, if a page has multiple independent search forms, MySearchView displays all of them and let the user choose which one to use by a simple click.

[12]Checked on January 5, 2010.

2. *Search form extraction*. Once the correct search form is identified, we can start to extract the desired information as listed in Table 4.1 from the search form. In most cases, this is a straightforward task as the name and location of the search engine server can be found from the *action* attribute, the HTTP request method can be found from the *method* attribute, and the name of each input control and its value can be identified from the *name* and *value* attributes of the *input tag*.

   In some cases, the action attributes of some search forms may not provide the full URL of the search engine server; instead, they may provide only a relative URL or no URL at all to the search engine server. In these cases, the search form extractor needs to construct the full URL that is required by HTTP request messages. Relative URLs may have two formats, one without a "/" (e.g., search.php) and one with "/" (e.g., /search.php). In the former case, the corresponding full URL can be constructed based on the current URL where the search form resides on and the relative URL. For example, suppose the current URL is `http://www.example.com/search/form.html` and the relative URL is search.php, then the full URL will be `http://www.example.com/search/search.php`. In the latter case, the corresponding full URL can be constructed by concatenating the *domain name* of the current URL, which is `http://www.example.com/` in our example, and the relative URL. For our example, the constructed full URL will be `http://www.example.com/search.php`. If no URL is specified in the action attribute, the full URL will be the same as the current URL.

   Sometimes, the *method* attribute may be absent in a search form. In this case, the *get* method is assumed as it is the default method in HTTP forms.

After the connection information for a search engine S as listed in Table 4.1 is obtained, the information can be plugged into a Java program template to generate the connector for S. Let `actionStr` denote the full location of the search engine server and `queryStr` denote the full query string (the name-value pairs of the input controls connected by &), including the user entered query. When the HTTP request method is *get*, the following are the Java statements that generate the new URL, establish the network connection and transmit the query to the search engine server, and receive the response page:

```
URL url = new URL(actionStr+"?"+ queryStr);
URLConnection yc = url.openConnection();
return yc.getInputStream();
```

When the HTTP request method is *post*, the following are the corresponding Java statements:

```
URL cgiUrl = new URL(actionStr);
URLConnection c = cgiUrl.openConnection();
c.setDoOutput(true);
c.setUseCaches(false);
c.setRequestProperty("Content-Type","application/x-
```

```
        www-form-urlencoded");
        DataOutputStream out = new
                DataOutputStream(c.getOutputStream());
        out.writeBytes(queryStr);
        System.out.println(queryStr);
        out.flush();
        out.close();
        return c.getInputStream();
```

Recently, some search engines use javascript to handle their search functions, which makes it more difficult to identify the connection information correctly. Generally, javascript could be used in two situations in a search interface: (i) It is used to generate the search form dynamically, and (ii) it is used to submit the search form. Systematic solutions are needed to extract search form parameters in both situations. As of today, we are not aware of any published solutions that deal with this challenge.

Note that the connection information of some search engines also includes cookies or session restrictions, which makes automatic construction of the connectors for these search engines even more challenging.

4.2 SEARCH RESULT EXTRACTION

As mentioned in Section 2.1, after a query is submitted to a component search engine, the search engine returns an initial response page. Search result records (SRRs) that are retrieved from the search engine are usually organized into multiple response pages. Each response page has a link to the next response page, if it exists. Response pages often also contain some unwanted information for the metasearch engine such as advertisements. Fig. 4.4 shows a portion of a response page from Lycos (`http://www.lycos.com/`) for query FIBA[13]. We can see that there are advertisement records above the regular SRRs and on the right portion of the response page. In fact, there are also advertisement records below the regular SRRs (not shown). It is important to correctly extract the SRRs on each response page. The program that performs SRR extraction is called an *extraction wrapper*. In this section, we review some selected techniques that can be used to produce extraction wrappers for search engines.

Some search engines, especially the large ones like Google and Yahoo!, provide APIs (application programming interfaces) or Web services interfaces, to allow applications to interact with their search engines. These interfaces usually provide specific means for applications to obtain the SRRs precisely. Unfortunately, most search engines do not provide such interfaces. Indeed, most search engines return SRRs in HTML pages. In this section, we focus on SRR extraction from HTML pages. As the response pages produced by different search engines usually have different formats, a separate SRR extraction wrapper needs to be generated for each search engine used.

[13]The query was submitted on September 1, 2010.

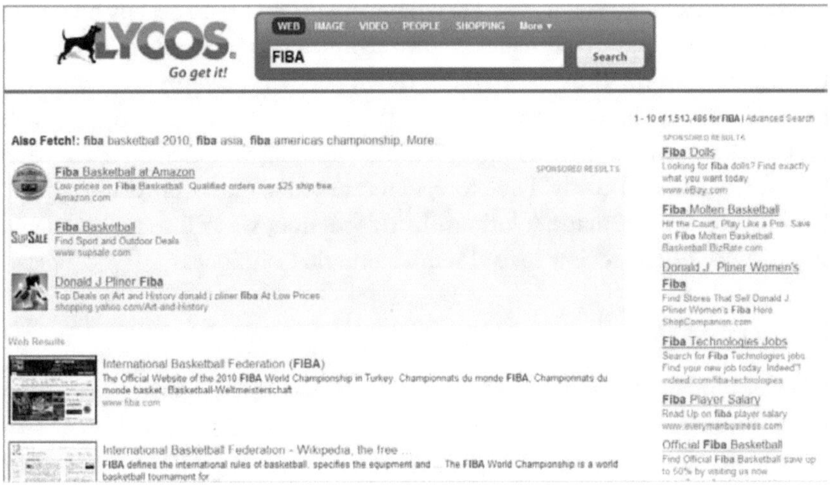

Figure 4.4: A Portion of a Response Page from Lycos.

SRR extraction is a special case of Web information extraction, which may extract other types of information such as products from Web pages. Two good surveys of Web information extraction techniques can be found in (Laender and Ribeiro-Neto, 2002; Chang et al., 2006). In this section, we will restrict our discussion to SRR extraction from HTML pages only.

Among the published SRR extraction techniques, some perform extraction for each response page from scratch without utilizing any saved knowledge about the response pages returned from the same search engine while others first generate the extraction rules based on sample response pages and then apply the rules to perform extraction for new response pages returned from the same search engine. The former type of methods is usually more time consuming and less robust because they need to perform all analyses from scratch and cannot utilize more robust knowledge that can be learned from sample response pages. As a result, this type of methods is less suitable for real-time applications that need accurate extraction of SRRs in a very timely manner. A metasearch engine is such an application. In contrast, the latter type of methods can usually yield faster and more accurate results. Therefore, in this section, we will emphasize techniques that generate extraction rules first, and we will call this type of approaches as *wrapper-based approaches*.

Wrapper-based approaches may be classified in different ways. One is by the degree of automation, i.e., to what degree the wrappers can be generated automatically. Based on this classification scheme, the methods can be classified into manual, semiautomatic, and automatic approaches. Manual techniques require an experienced developer to manually analyze the HTML source files of several response pages from the same search engine and identify the patterns or rules for extracting SRRs. Semiautomatic methods often require a human to manually mark the correct SRRs on several response pages; then, the wrapper generation system induces the extraction rules based on the human input. Automatic techniques can generate wrappers without requiring any human involvement. Both manual and semiautomatic techniques involve significant manual effort. Furthermore, manual methods can only be performed by experienced developers with strong programming skills. It is known that search engines change their result display format from time to time, which may cause existing wrappers to become useless. Creating and maintaining wrappers manually and semiautomatically are inconvenient and costly. Therefore, in recent years, most efforts in wrapper generation techniques are focused on automatic solutions. In this section, we will focus mostly on automatic solutions. But, first, we briefly review several semiautomatic techniques.

4.2.1 SEMIAUTOMATIC WRAPPER GENERATION

A large number of semiautomatic wrapper generation methods and systems have been developed such as WIEN (Kushmerick, N., 1997; Kushmerick et al., 1997), SoftMealy (Hsu and Dung, 1998), Stalker (Muslea et al., 1999), Lixto (Baumgartner et al., 2001b), and Thresher (Hogue and Karger, 2005). A survey of these approaches can be found in (Chang et al., 2006). These approaches are also called *supervised extraction techniques*. These techniques were not specifically designed to extract SRRs from search engine returned response pages, but they are potentially applicable to SRR extraction. In this section, we provide a brief review of several of these techniques.

WIEN

WIEN stands for *wrapper induction environment* (Kushmerick, N., 1997) that supports a family of wrapper classes mostly designed for extracting data records in tabular format. Each data record consists of values belonging to different attributes such as title and author for books. SRRs returned by search engines can be viewed as data records with several attributes such as title, snippet and URL. One of the wrapper classes supported by WIEN is HLRT (head-left-right-tail), which performs data record extraction using a number of delimiters. Specifically, if each data record has k values, then $2^*k + 2$ delimiters are needed: a head delimiter that separates any contents above the first record, a tail delimiter that separates any contents below the last record, and a pair of delimiters for the values of each attribute, one on the left and one on the right. If there are irrelevant contents between different data records, then another wrapper class HOCLRT (head-opening-closing-left-right-tail) can be used. The difference between HOCLRT and HLRT is that the former has an extra pair of delimiters for each data record, one opening delimiter before each data record and one closing delimiter after each data record.

Kushmerick, N. (1997) determines the delimiters in each wrapper class by induction based on a set of labeled response pages. Each labeled page has clearly identified data records and their values. During induction, any common suffix of the strings preceding the values of the i-th attribute is a possible candidate of the left delimiter of the i-th attribute, and any common prefix of the strings following the values of the i-th attribute is a possible candidate of the right delimiter of the i-th attribute. Similarly, candidates of head delimiters, tail delimiters, opening delimiters, and closing delimiters can also be identified, although the process is more complicated. Then the wrapper induction system enumerates all combinations of these candidates for all the delimiters until a *consistent wrapper* is produced. A wrapper is said to be consistent with a labeled page if it can extract all the data records and attribute values on the page correctly.

Lixto

Lixto (Baumgartner et al., 2001a,b) is a semiautomatic wrapper generation tool designed to extract information from HTML documents and represent the extracted information in XML format. Once a wrapper is created, it can be used to extract the same type of information from similarly formatted HTML documents automatically.

Lixto provides a graphical and interactive user interface for users to create wrappers. The basic procedure a user (i.e., a wrapper designer) can follow to create a wrapper is as follows. First, the user opens an example Web page that contains desired information, e.g., a response page returned by a search engine. This essentially loads the page to Lixto's special browser, which makes the page contents markable using the mouse of a computer. Next, the user adds some *patterns* to extract desired information. Each pattern is given a name that will be used as the corresponding element name for the extracted information in XML. For example, *ResultRecords* could be used as the pattern name for SRRs. Each pattern consists of one or more *filters* and each filter in turn consists of some conditions. Each instance of the desired information (e.g., an SRR) must satisfy all conditions of at least one filter of the pattern.

When creating a filter, the user marks an instance of the desired information using the mouse. Based on the marked instance, Lixto first analyzes the features of the instance (e.g., font type) and its delimiters to create the conditions of the filter, and then shows all instances on the input Web page that match the filter. At this time, one of the following three possibilities will occur. First, all desired instances are matched and no undesired information is matched. This indicates that this filter is correct and can be saved for later use. Second, some desired instances are not matched. In this case, the user will attempt to create another filter by marking a desired instance that was not matched by the previously created filter(s). This process of creating additional filters is repeated until all desired instances can be matched. Third, some undesired information is matched. In this case, some conditions will be added to this filter to make the extraction more precise. For example, if undesired information before the first desired instance FI is matched, a restrictive condition can be added to express that certain element must appear immediately before FI to make it impossible for the undesired information to match the filter. In general, conditions can be added to a filter to restrict match, and filters can be added to a pattern to increase match iteratively until perfect extraction of all desired instances is achieved.

Internally, in Lixto, each wrapper consists of one or more patterns. Each pattern is a set of extraction rules and each rule is expressed in a datalog-like language called *Elog*. Each rule basically corresponds to a filter and the conditions of the filter are expressed as different types of predicate atoms in the rule. For example, in the following rule for identifying a price value (Baumgartner et al.,

2001a):

$$\text{pricewc}(S, X) \leftarrow \text{price}(\_, S), \text{subtext}(S, [0-9]^{+}\backslash.[0-9]^{+}, X),$$

there are two predicate atoms: The first one (i.e., price(_, S)) specifies the context S of the extraction (the context itself is defined by another rule) and the second one specifies the pattern of a price within the given context. The rules in different patterns are automatically generated based on user-marked contents on the input Web page as well as information provided by the user during the interactive process.

Thresher

Thresher is a tool that allows non-technical users to extract desired contents from Web pages (Hogue and Karger, 2005). Basically, it allows a user to mark and annotate desired Web contents off a browser (the Haystack semantic Web browser from MIT (Quan et al., 2003) was used by Thresher). The annotations help obtain the semantics of the desired contents. Thresher was specifically designed for Web pages that contain many objects of the same type. Thus, it is very suitable for SRR extraction as SRRs on response pages returned from the same search engine can be considered as this type of objects.

In using Thresher, a user first uses the mouse to mark some desired objects on the input Web page. Thresher then induces a wrapper to extract all similar objects on the page. If needed, the user may mark more examples, even from different pages, to improve the accuracy of the wrapper until the user is satisfied. The user can then annotate data items of some sample objects with semantic labels (e.g., annotating the titles of SRRs as "title") in an interactive manner. Once a wrapper is induced by Thresher, it can be used to extract similar objects and their semantic information from other similar pages. The learned wrappers are in RDF (resource description framework) format so they can be easily shared.

Wrapper induction in Thresher is carried out by learning a tree template pattern from the user-marked example objects. Each marked object corresponds to a subtree in the DOM (Document Object Model) tree of the page. From the subtrees of the marked objects, Thresher looks for the strictest tree pattern that matches all marked objects. In order to find this tree pattern, and knowing that the layout of different objects may be different due to their difference in content, the corresponding elements in these subtrees need to be properly mapped. Thresher finds the best element mapping using *tree edit distance*, i.e., the mapping that yields the lowest-cost tree edit distance is selected. Here the tree edit distance from tree T_1 to tree T_2 is the minimum cost of all sequences of edit operations that transform T_1 to T_2 (Tai, K., 1979) using the following allowable edit operations: (1) Change one node into another node, (2) delete one node from a tree, and (3) insert a node into a tree.

Once the best mapping is found, the tree pattern is generated by starting from the subtree of one of the marked objects and replacing any nodes that do not match in the subtrees of other marked objects with wildcard nodes. In Fig. 4.5 (a) and (b), the subtrees of two objects and their mappings (dashed lines) are shown. Assuming that all the texts are different, then Fig. 4.5 (c) represents the tree pattern after unmatched notes have been replaced by wildcards (denoted as a circle with * in it). Furthermore, highly similar neighboring elements can be collapsed into a single wildcard node, yielding the final tree pattern as shown in Fig. 4.5 (d).

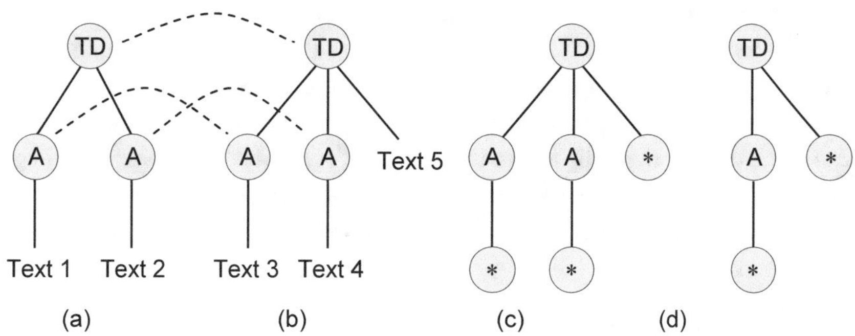

Figure 4.5: Illustrating Tree Pattern Generation.

4.2.2 AUTOMATIC WRAPPER GENERATION

In recent years, more research effort has been focused on developing fully automatic Web information extraction techniques. These techniques are also known as unsupervised techniques as they require no human involvement. This type of techniques can only be applied to Web pages with multiple objects of the same type because the presence of multiple similarly structured objects makes it possible to discover the repeating pattern among these objects.

The following three types of information have been used to perform automatic wrapper generation in different approaches.

- *Tag information*. Contents in HTML documents are wrapped in HTML tags. Each HTML document can be either represented as a string of tags and text tokens or as a DOM/tag tree. The tree representation captures more structures (e.g., nested structure) among the tags than the string representation. Both of these representations have been used by earlier automatic wrapper generation techniques, such as RoadRunner (Crescenzi et al., 2001), Omini (Buttler et al., 2001), DeLA (Wang and Lochovsky, 2003), and EXALG (Arasu and Garcia-Molina, 2003).

- *Visual information*. When an HTML document is rendered on a browser, rich visual information becomes available such as the size and location of each section, the size and location of images, the colors of different types of texts, the gap between different SRRs, etc. In recent years, tools that can obtain different types of visual information and feed them to applications have been developed, which make it possible to utilize such visual information in wrapper generation systems automatically. As a result, in recent years, several methods have explored utilizing the visual information on rendered Web pages to perform data extraction. Most of these systems use visual information together with tag structures and these systems include ViNTs (Zhao et al., 2005), ViPER (Simon and Lausen, 2005), and DEPTA (Zhai and Liu, 2006).

There are several reasons that make it very difficult to derive accurate wrappers based on HTML tags alone (Yang and Zhang, 2001; Zhao et al., 2005). For example, HTML tags are often used in unexpected ways, which means that not much convention on tag usage can be reliably utilized in wrapper generation. In addition, today's Web browsers are very robust, and they can often display many ill-formed Web pages "perfectly." However, such ill-formed Web pages may cause problems to wrapper generators. Utilizing visual information on Web pages can overcome some of the problems with HTML tags and can also take advantage of today's robust browsers.

Recently, an automatic wrapper generation system, ViDRE, that uses only visual information on Web pages has been proposed (Liu et al., 2010). There are advantages of using only visual information to perform wrapper generation. It reduces or even eliminates reliance on analyzing HTML source code of Web pages. Note that HTML is still evolving (from version 2.0 to the current version 4.01, and version 5.0 is being drafted). When HTML changes, HTML-based wrapper generation techniques may also need to change. Furthermore, HTML is no longer the exclusive Web page programming language, and other languages have been introduced, such as XHTML and XML. A visual-based Web language independent solution will not be affected by these changes.

- *Domain information*. Some search engines, especially Web databases, search information from specific domains such as books, cars, etc. Useful domain knowledge can be collected for each domain and organized into domain ontology to facilitate the extraction of SRRs returned from search engines in the domain. Domain information is usually used together with other types of information such as tag information to perform wrapper generation. An earlier method used manually created domain ontologies (Embley et al., 1999) while the ODE system (Su et al., 2009) created ontologies automatically, making ODE a fully automatic solution. Some visual features are also utilized by ODE.

In this section, we introduce several automatic wrapper generation systems in more detail. These systems include Omini (Buttler et al., 2001), ViNTs (Zhao et al., 2005), ODE (Su et al., 2009) and ViDRE (Liu et al., 2010). Among these systems, Omini uses only tag information, ViNTs uses both tag information and visual information, ODE uses tag information, visual information and domain information, and ViDRE uses only visual information. These systems are either specifically designed for extracting SRRs from response pages returned by search engines (including Web databases that search more structured data records stored in backend database systems) or with such an application as a primary consideration. To simplify presentation, we will use SRRs uniformly as the extraction target in describing these systems. A common feature of these systems is that, during

SRR extraction, they all try to identify the *query result section* on the input response page first and to extract the SRRs in the query result section afterwards.

Omini

Omini is one of the earliest automatic wrapper generation systems for extracting objects (SRRs) from Web pages (Buttler et al., 2001). Omini performs SRR extraction by analyzing the patterns of the tag tree of the input query response page, and it consists of three steps. Step 1 identifies the *minimal subtree* in the tag tree that contains all desired SRRs. This is equivalent to identifying the query result section that contains all the SRRs. Step 2 identifies the SRR separator that can segment the query result section into SRRs. The identified separator may be imperfect which may cause problems such as breaking an SRR into multiple pieces or extracting extraneous SRRs. Step 3 extracts the SRRs from the query result section using the identified separator while taking into consideration the possibility that the separator is not perfect. More details of these steps are given below.

Step 1: Query result section identification. To identify the minimal subtree that contains all the SRRs in the tag tree of the response page, Omini combines the following three subtree discovery heuristics, i.e., the minimal subtree is usually the subtree that (1) is rooted at the node with the highest fanout (i.e., the node with the largest number of child nodes); (2) has the largest content size in byte; and (3) has the largest number of tags.

Step 2: SRR separator discovery. First, Omini limits the search of the correct separator among the child tags of the root of the minimal subtree. In other words, only these tags will be considered as candidate separators, and we will call them *candidate tags*. Next, Omini employs the following five heuristics to rank candidate tags as the possible separator.

- *Standard deviation heuristic.* For each candidate tag, this heuristic measures the standard deviation in the number of characters between two consecutive occurrences of the tag (only starting tags are counted). Omini ranks the candidate tags in ascending order of the standard deviation based on the observation that SRRs returned by the same search engine have similar sizes and the requirement that the same separator tag is used to separate all SRRs.

- *Repeating pattern heuristic.* For each pair of adjacent tags with no text in between, this heuristic computes the difference between the count of this tag pair and the count of each of the two tags in the pair. If the difference is zero for a pair, it means that the two tags always appear together. Omini ranks the pairs in ascending order of the count difference based on the intuition that tag pairs have stronger meaning than individual tags.

- *Identifiable path separator (IPS) tag heuristic.* IPS tags are those HTML tags that are widely used to separate different SRRs such as table row tag < tr >, paragraph tag <p>, and list tag < li >. Omini computes the percentage of times each tag is used as an SRR separator in a set of sample Web pages and then ranks the tags in descending order of their percentages.

- *Sibling tag heuristic*. This heuristic counts pairs of tags that are immediate siblings in the minimal subtree and ranks the tag pairs in descending order of the counts. If two pairs have the same count, the one that appears first is preferred. This heuristic is motivated by the observations that, given a minimal subtree, the separator should appear the same number of times as the SRRs, and that tag pairs have stronger meanings than individual tags.

- *Partial path heuristic*. This heuristic identifies all tag paths from each candidate tag to any reachable node in the subtree rooted at the candidate tag and ranks candidate tags in descending order of the number of identical paths from them. If two tags have the same number of partial paths, the one with the longer path is preferred. This heuristic is based on the observation that the SRRs returned by the same search engine usually have similar tag structures.

Omini employs a probabilistic method to combine the five heuristics into an integrated solution. Specifically, Omini first estimates the *success rate* of each heuristic based on a set of sample pages (it is the percentage of the sample pages in which the top-ranked candidate separator of the heuristic is correct), then evaluates the overall success rates of different combinations of the five heuristics based on the assumption that the heuristics are independent. The evaluation determined that the combination using all of the five heuristics has the best performance (Buttler et al., 2001).

Omini's SRR separator discovery method was heavily influenced by an earlier work (Embley et al., 1999). The first two heuristics used in Omini's solution were first proposed in the earlier work, and the third heuristic was revised from a heuristic in the earlier work.

Step 3: SRR extraction. Once the SRR separator is identified, it is straightforward to use it to segment the query result section into SRRs. However, it is possible that the separator is not perfect, which leads to some incorrectly extracted SRRs. Two problematic situations are identified (Buttler et al., 2001). The first is that an SRR may have been broken into multiple pieces by the separator. In this case, these pieces need to be merged together to construct the SRR. The second is that some extraneous SRRs (e.g., advertisements) may have been extracted. Omini identifies extraneous SRRs by looking for SRRs that are different from the majority of the extracted SRRs, for having either a different set of tags or different sizes. The possibility that multiple SRRs may have been incorrectly grouped into a single SRR was not addressed in this work.

Wrapper rules were not explicitly discussed by Buttler et al. (2001), but it is easy to see that the tag path to the root of the minimal subtree and the SRR separator tag identified for a response page returned by a search engine can be stored as the extraction wrapper for extracting SRRs from new response pages returned by the same search engine.

ViNTs

ViNTs (Zhao et al., 2005) is an automatic wrapper generator that was specifically designed to extract SRRs from search engine returned response pages. It is also one of the earliest automatic wrapper generators that utilize both the visual information on response pages and the tag structures of the HTML source documents to generate wrappers. ViNTs makes use of visual features and tag structures as follows. It first uses visual features to identify candidate SRRs. It then derives candidate wrappers from the tag paths related to the candidate SRRs. Finally, it selects the most promising wrapper using both visual features and tag structures.

ViNTs takes one or more sample response pages from a search engine as input and generate a wrapper for extracting the SRRs from new response pages returned from the same search engine as output. The sample response pages can be automatically generated by the system through submitting automatically generated sample queries to the search engine. For each input sample response page, its tag tree is built to analyze its tag structures and the page itself is rendered on a browser to extract its visual information.

Content-line is the basic building block of the ViNTs approach. It is a group of characters that visually form a horizontal line in the same section on the rendered page. In ViNTs, eight types of content lines are differentiated, such as link line (the line is the anchor text of a hyperlink), text line, link-text line (has both text and link), blank line, and so on. A code is assigned to each type of content lines, called the *type code*. Each content line has a rendering box, and the left x coordinate of the rendering box is called the *position code* of the content line. Thus, each content line is represented as a (type code, position code) pair.

Example 4.1 In Fig. 4.6, the first SRR has 5 content lines, the first line is a link line with type code 1, the second and third lines are text lines with type code 2 (in ViNTs, adjacent content lines of the same type are merged into a single line, which means that the second and third content lines will be treated as a single text line), the fourth line is a link-text line with type code 3, and the fifth line is a blank line with type code 8. All these lines have the same position code, say 50, as no line is indented.

L1:
Metasearch Engine Project
L2:
This project was sponsored by research grants from the National Science Foundation .
Principal Investigator at SUNY at Binghamton PI: Prof. Weiyi Meng
L3:
www.cs.binghamton.edu/~meng/metasearch.html - Cached
L4:
L5:
Web Database Metasearch Engine Project
L6:
Collaborative Research Achieving Information Integration of Web Databases Through the
Construction of Metasearch Engines
L7:
www.cs.binghamton.edu/~meng/DMSE.html - Cached
L8:
L9:
Project Ideas: MetaSearch Engine
L10:
Project Ideas |Computer Project Ideas | Engineering Project | Science Fair Project
Ideas | School Projects | Project Download | Electronics | Mechanical | IT | Electrical ...
L11:
iprojectideas.blogspot.com/2010/07/metasearch-engine.html - Cached
L12:

Figure 4.6: A Segment of a Sample Response Page.

To remove useless content lines from a sample response page, another response page for a non-existing query string, called *no-result page*, is utilized. Basically, those content lines in the sample response page that also appear in the no-result page are removed.

The remaining content lines are grouped into *blocks* based on *candidate content line separators* (CCLSs) that are content lines appearing at least three times. ViNTs requires each sample response page used for wrapper generation to contain at least four SRRs. Each CCLS may contain one or more consecutive content lines, and the content lines of a CCLS are the ending part of each block.

Example 4.2 Consider Fig. 4.6. If blank line is a CCLS or link-text line followed by blank line together form a CCLS, the yielded blocks will correspond to the correct SRRs. However, when link line is a CCLS, the following blocks will be formed: (L1), (L2, L3, L4, L5), (L6, L7, L8, L9). Note that (L10, L11, L12) do not form a block as the last line is not a link line.

In ViNTs, each block is characterized by three features: *type code* – the sequence of type codes of the content lines of the block, *position code* – the smallest x coordinate of the block that is closest to the left boundary of the rendered page, and *shape code* – the ordered list of the position codes of the content lines of the block. Given two blocks, distances between their type codes, position codes, and shape codes can be defined. Two blocks are visually similar, if these distances are all below their respective thresholds.

Each CCLS that yields a sequence of visually similar blocks is kept. Such a sequence of blocks is called a *block group*. Intuitively, each block group corresponds to a section on the response page. There may be multiple such sections, for example, one for the real SRRs (i.e., the query result section) and one or more for advertisement records. In general, these blocks do not necessarily correspond to the actual SRRs. For example, when link line is used as a CCLS in Fig. 4.6, two produced blocks, i.e., (L2, L3, L4, L5) and (L6, L7, L8, L9), are visually similar, but they do not correspond to actual SRRs.To find the blocks that correspond to the correct records, ViNTs identifies the *first line* of each SRR in each of the current blocks. These first lines in different blocks repartitions the content lines in each section into new blocks. ViNTs uses several heuristic rules to identify the first line of a record from a given block. For example, two of these heuristic rules are (1) the only content line that starts with a number is a first line; and (2) if there is only one blank line in a block, the line immediately following the blank line is the first line. For the example in Fig. 4.6, the link line immediately following the blank line in each block will be identified as the first line.

Based on the new blocks in each block group, ViNTs generates a *candidate wrapper* from the tag paths from the root of the tag tree to beginning of each new block in the block group. In ViNTs, wrappers are regular expressions of the format: *prefix* (*X* (*separator1* | *separator2* | …))[min, max], where *prefix* is a tag path, X is a wildcard for any sequence of tags representing subtrees rooted at these tags (called *sub-forest*) of the *tag tree* of the response page, each *separator* is also a sequence of tags representing a sub-forest of the tag tree[14], "|" is *the alternation operator*, the concatenation of X

[14]Note that the tag-based separators here are different from the content line based separators (i.e., CCLSs) that are used earlier for content line partition. Sometimes more than one separator may be needed (Zhao et al., 2005).

and a separator corresponds to a record (i.e., each occurrence of the child sub-forest rooted at the tags in X and a separator corresponds to a record), min and max are used to select SRRs within a range from a list of SRRs (usually, min and max are set to 1 and the maximum number of records that may appear in a response page, respectively). The *prefix* determines the *minimal subtree t* that contains all records in the block group. The separators are used to segment all descendants of t into records. The following example illustrates how the *prefix* and *separator* are derived from a sequence of tag paths, from the root of the tag tree to the beginning of each block, in a block group. Each tag path is sequence of *tag nodes*, and each tag node consists of a tag followed by a *direction code*, which can be either C or S (Zhao et al., 2005). Tag node <t>C and <t>S mean, respectively, that the next tag following this tag node is the first child tag and the first sibling tag of tag <t> in the tag tree.

Example 4.3 Consider the following four tag paths for three consecutive blocks:
P_1: < html >C< head >S< body >C< img >S< center >S< hr > S<b>S< hr >
S< dl >C< dt >C< strong >C<a>C
P_2: < html >C< head >S< body >C< img >S< center >S< hr >S<b>S< hr >
S< font >S<dl>S< dl>C< dt >C< strong >C<a>C
P_3: < html >C< head >S< body >C< img >S< center >S< hr > S< b > S< hr >
S< font >S< dl >S<dl>S< dl >C< dt >C< strong >C<a>C
P_4: < html >C< head >S< body >C< img >S< center >S< hr >S<b>S< hr >
S< font >S< dl >S<dl>S<font>S<dl >S< dl >C< dt >C< strong >C<a>C
The < font > tags are used to achieve the effect that adjacent records are displayed in different colors. For this example, prefix is the maximum common prefix of these tag paths, i.e., prefix = < html >C< head >S< body >C< img >S< center >S< hr >S<b>S< hr >S. The separator can be derived as follows. First, subtract prefix from each tag path. Let $PF_i = P_i$ – prefix for $i = 1, \ldots, 4$. Next, remove all C nodes from the end of each PFi (the reason for doing so is that the tag structures of SRRs are siblings under the same minimum sub-tree). Then, compute $Diff_i = PF_{i+1} - PF_i$ for $i = 1, \ldots, 3$. We have $Diff_1 =< font > S < dl > S$, $Diff_2 =< dl > S$ and $Diff_3 =< font > S < dl > S$. The common suffix in these Diffs is < dl >S and the tag (sequence) in this common suffix is the separator, which is < df > for this example. Furthermore, for this example, X is either empty or < font >. In the former case, in the minimal subtree, each child subtree rooted at $< dl >$ corresponds to a record. In the latter case, each child sub-forest consisting of the subtrees rooted at $< font >$ and $< dl >$ corresponds to a record.

If there are K block groups (sections) on a response page, then K candidate wrappers will be produced, one for each group. Search engines usually display their SRRs in one section. Therefore, if $K > 1$, then one of these wrappers need to be selected as the wrapper for the input response page. ViNTs performs this selection using several heuristics, including the size of the corresponding section (the query result section usually has the largest area compared to other sections), the location of the section (the query result section is usually centrally located on the response page), and so on.

Many search engines do not always display their search results in the same exact format. To increase the likelihood of capturing all varieties, multiple sample response pages from the same search engine should be used to generate the wrapper. For each sample page, the process described above is followed to generate a wrapper for the page. Then the wrappers for different sample pages are integrated into a single and more robust wrapper for the search engine. Wrapper integration in ViNTs consists of prefix integration, separator integration and [min, max] integration.

ViNTs was used to generate wrappers for most of the search engines used in the AllInOneNews metasearch engine (Liu et al., 2007).

ODE

ODE (Su et al., 2009) is an ontology-assisted data extraction system that is also specifically designed to extract SRRs from response pages returned by Web databases. ODE first constructs an ontology for a domain. Then, it uses the constructed domain ontology to perform SRR extraction. ODE can also align and label data items within SRRs (i.e., put values corresponding to the same attribute into the same group and assign a semantic label to each group) using the constructed domain ontology. In fact, data item alignment and label assignment can benefit most from the constructed ontology although the ontology is also useful in identifying the query result section that contains SRRs. Here we will mostly focus on the part related to SRR extraction.

In ODE, a *domain ontology* is a data model that describes a set of concepts within the domain and the relationships between those concepts. It consists of an *ontology attribute model* that describes the organization of the attributes of the objects within the domain and an *attribute description* that contains the values of each attribute in the ontology. An ontology attribute model for the book domain is shown in Fig. 4.7 (a), and an attribute description for the price attribute in the book domain is shown in Fig. 4.7 (b) Su et al. (2009). In Fig. 4.7 (a), the solid-line rectangle indicates the book object, the dotted-line rectangles represent the attributes of the object, and arrows indicate the *part-of relationships* between attributes. As can be seen from Fig. 4.7 (b), each attribute A has the following fields: *name*, *alias*(*es*), *data type*, *external representation*(*s*) of A's value in a response page (e.g., a regular expression for the values of A), *values* of A that appear in the sample response pages, *value probability*, which is the likelihood that an attribute value occurs in an SRR, *name probability*, which is the likelihood that the name or one of its aliases occurs in an SRR in a response page, and *max occurrence*, which is the maximum number of occurrences of A's values within an SRR in the sample response pages. Each domain ontology in ODE is automatically constructed using the query interfaces and some sample response pages from Web databases in the domain.

ODE performs SRR extraction in two steps: (1) *Query result section identification*. This step identifies the section that contains the valid SRRs. (2) *Record segmentation*. This step segments the query result section into SRRs. Wrapper generation and wrapper format in ODE are not explicitly discussed. Among the above two steps, only the first step utilizes the domain ontology. The main ideas of the above two steps are summarized below.

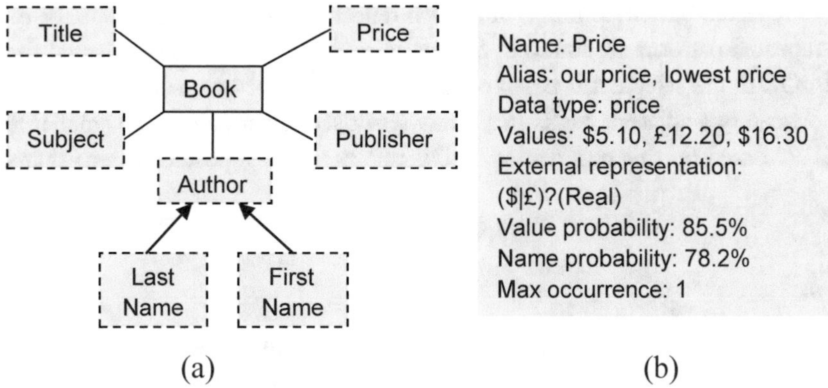

Figure 4.7: (a) Ontology attribute model for the book domain. (b) Attribute description for the Price attribute in the book domain.

Step 1: Query result section identification. In this step, ODE first employs a tag tree based method called PADE to identify the query result section. However, PADE may fail to identify the correct query result section; for example, it is possible that the records in the identified section are not valid SRRs, or no section is identified because fewer than two similar records appear on the input response page. ODE improves PADE by recognizing the PADE produced section as the correct query result section only if the content of the section has sufficiently high (as determined by a threshold) correlation with the domain ontology. The correlation between a record R (not necessarily a valid SRR) in a section and the domain ontology is a normalized sum of the weights measuring the match between each string in R and the information in the *attribute descriptions* of the attributes in the domain ontology. If the string matches the name or an alias of an attribute, the weight is the *name probability* of the attribute (see Fig. 4.7 (b)); otherwise, if the string matches a value of several attributes, then the weight is the largest of the *value probabilities* of these attributes. If the PADE produced section does not satisfy the correlation condition, other sections will be examined. If no section is identified by PADE, ODE finds the subtree with the highest correlation with the ontology. If the correlation is higher than a threshold, ODE returns the subtree as a single SRR. If no qualified subtree can be found, ODE assumes there is no valid SRR on the input response page. Note that in the latter two cases, no separate step for SRR extraction is needed.

Step 2: Record segmentation. This step is to segment the query result section into SRRs. In ODE, ontology is not used for this step. In this step, each query result section S is represented as a string consisting of HTML tags and special tokens (e.g., text contents are denoted by token *text*). ODE first finds continuous repeated patterns (called *C-repeated patterns*) from the string (Wang and Lochovsky, 2003). Each C-repeated pattern is a repeated substring of S having at least two adjacent occurrences. As an example, in the string ABABABA, there are two C-repeated patterns: AB and BA.

If only one C-repeated pattern is found in S, each repeat of the pattern corresponds to an SRR. If multiple C-repeated patterns are found in S, then one of them needs to be selected for identifying the SRRs. In ODE, the selection is based on the following observation (Zhai and Liu, 2006): The visual gap between two adjacent SRRs in a query result section should be no smaller than any gap within an SRR. Based on this observation, ODE selects the C-repeated pattern that satisfies this condition.

ViDRE

ViDRE is part of ViDE (Liu et al., 2010) that is specifically developed to extract SRRs from response pages returned from Web databases. ViDRE is the first published method that uses only visual information on rendered Web pages to perform automatic record-level wrapper generation.

Similar to other wrapper generation approaches, ViDRE also uses sample Web pages to build wrappers. From a sample response page, ViDRE uses the VIPS algorithm to generate a *visual block tree* (Cai et al., 2003). A visual block tree for a Web page is basically a segmentation of the page. The root block represents the whole page, and each block in the tree corresponds to a rectangular region on the page. The leaf blocks are the blocks that cannot be segmented further, and they represent the minimum semantic units, such as continuous texts or images. If each SRR corresponds to a database record, then a non-image leaf block typically corresponds to an attribute value. In a visual block tree, block A contains block B if A is an ancestor of B. Two blocks do not overlap unless one of them contains the other. The order of the sibling blocks from left to right with the same parent is significant.

In ViDRE, each internal node A in the visual block tree is represented by $A = (CS, P, S, FS, IS)$, where CS is the list of child blocks of A, P is its position (i.e., the coordinates of the upper-left corner of the block on the rendered page), S is its size (height and width), FS is the set of fonts used in A, and IS is the number of images in A. Each leaf node B is represented by $B = (P, S, F, L, I, C)$, where P and S are the same as the P and S for an internal node, F is its font, L indicates whether B is a hyperlink text, I indicates whether B is an image, and C is its content if B is a text.

ViDRE uses four types of visual features to perform SRR extraction. These features are shown in Table 4.2.

Given one or more sample response pages returned by a Web database, ViDRE generates the wrapper for the Web database in three main steps: (1) *Query result section identification.* This step identifies the section that contains all SRRs. (2) *SRR extraction.* This step extracts the SRRs from the identified query result section. (3) *Wrapper generation.* This step generates the wrapper for extracting the SRRs from response pages returned by the Web database. These three steps are briefly described below.

Step 1: Query result section identification. Position and size features are used to locate the block corresponding to the query result section. First, PF1 is used to identify all blocks that are centered horizontally. Next, PF2 is used to determine the correct block. In ViDRE, if the ratio of the size of

Table 4.2: Different Types of Visual Features.

Position features (PFs). These features indicate the location of the query result section on a response page.
PF1: Query result sections are always centered horizontally.
PF2: The size of the query result section is usually large relative to the area size of the whole page. (This is actually a size feature.)
Layout features (LFs). These features indicate how SRRs in the query result section are typically arranged.
LF1: The SRRs are usually aligned flush left in the query result section.
LF2: All SRRs are adjoining.
LF3: Adjoining SRRs do not overlap, and the gap space between any two adjoining SRRs is the same.
Appearance features (AFs). These features capture the visual features within SRRs.
AF1: SRRs are very similar in their appearances, and the similarity includes the sizes of the images they contain and the fonts they use.
AF2: The data items of the same semantic (e.g., values under the same attribute) in different SRRs have similar presentations with respect to position, size (image data item), and font (text data item).
AF3: The neighboring text data items of different semantics often (not always) use distinguishable fonts.
Content features (CFs). These features hint the regularity of the contents in SRRs.
CF1: The first data item in each SRR is always of a mandatory type (i.e., it must have non-null value).
CF2: The presentation of data items in SRRs follows a fixed order (e.g., title precedes author in all SRRs).

a horizontally centered block to the size of whole response page is greater than or equal to 0.4, then the section corresponding to the block is recognized as the query result section.

Step 2: SRR extraction. This step has three phases. In Phase 1, some noise blocks that cannot be SRRs are filtered out. Based on LF2, noise blocks can only appear at the top or bottom of the query result section. Thus, blocks located at these two locations should be examined. Based on LF1, if a block at these positions is not aligned flush left, it is removed as a noise block. In Phase 2, the goal is to group the remaining leaf blocks based on their semantics, i.e., each non-image group should correspond to the values of the same attribute in different SRRs. By AF2 and AF3, this goal can be achieved by clustering the leaf blocks based on their *appearance similarity*. The *appearance similarity* between two leaf blocks in ViDRE is computed as a weighted sum of the similarities based on the image sizes, plain text fonts, and link text fonts of the two blocks, respectively. In Phase 3, SRRs are generated by regrouping the leaf blocks such that each new group consists of the blocks belonging to the same SRR. To avoid confusion, groups generated in Phase 2 will be called *c-groups* (i.e., *column groups* as each such group corresponds to a column of a table, namely, it consists of the values of an attribute) and the new groups to be generated in Phase 3 will be called *r-groups* (i.e., *row groups*). The basic idea of block regrouping is as follows. First, select a c-group with the maximum number of blocks and use these blocks as seeds to grow r-groups (i.e., SRRs). According to CF1, the c-group containing the first data item (attribute value) in each SRR satisfies this condition. Let G denote this c-group. Then, for each block from c-groups, determine the r-group to which the block belongs and add this block to this r-group. Let b^* be a block from another c-group G^*. The basic idea for finding a right r-group for b^* is to identify the block b among the blocks in G such that b^* should be assigned to the same r-group as b. This desired b is the block in G that has the smallest vertical distance (in terms of the y coordinates of the two blocks) from b^* and does not appear below b^* because b^* should be either in the same row as b or below b (not necessarily directly) as b is the block corresponding to the first attribute value in the SRR (r-group).

Step 3: Wrapper generation. Given a response page P, the wrapper generated by ViDRE consists of information for locating the correct query result section S in the visual block tree and information for extracting the SRRs from the child blocks of S. The wrapper information for S is represented by five values (x, y, w, h, l), where x and y are the coordinates of the upper left corner of S on P, w and h are the width and height of S, and l is the level of S in the visual block tree. Given a new response page P^*, the system first checks the blocks at level l in the visual block tree for P^* and among these blocks, the one that has the largest area overlap with the query result section S of P is recognized as the query result section on P^*. The underlying assumption here is that the level of query result sections in visual block trees remain unchanged for different response pages of the same search engine. The overlap area can be computed using the coordinates and width/height information of the two blocks under consideration.

The wrapper information for SRR extraction contains the visual information (plain text fonts, link text fonts or image size, depending on the type of block) of the first block (i.e., first data item or attribute value) of each SRR extracted from P and the gap space (denoted as g) between two adjacent SRRs. For the child blocks of the query result section in P^*, the system first finds the first block of each SRR by the visual similarity with the saved visual information (i.e., plain text fonts, link text fonts or image size, depending on the type of block), and then utilizes LF3 (i.e., the gap space between each pair of valid adjacent SRRS is the same) to identify all SRRS in the query result section in P^*.

CHAPTER 5

Result Merging

The goal of the result merging component is to merge the search result records (SRRs) returned by different search engines into a single ranked list. Many result merging algorithms have been proposed and studied since 1990's. These algorithms can be classified along several dimensions. For example, one dimension is the amount of information about each result that is used to perform the merging. This may range from using only the local ranks of each result from the search engines that retrieved it, to using the SRR of the result, and to using the full document of the result. Another dimension is the degree of overlap of the documents among the search engines used to answer a query. This can range from no overlap, to partial overlap, and to possibly identical document collections.

Early result merging algorithms assumed that all component search engines return a local similarity for each retrieved result with respect to the given user query (Callan et al., 1995; Dreilinger and Howe, 1997; Gauch et al., 1996; Selberg and Etzioni, 1997). Local similarities may not be directly comparable due to several reasons. For example, one reason is that different component search engines may normalize their similarities into different ranges, e.g., one in [0, 1] and another in [0, 1000]. Another reason is that term weights of documents in different search engines are computed based on different collection statistics (e.g., document frequency).

To make the local similarities more comparable, the merging algorithm re-normalize local similarities into a common range, for example, [0, 1]. A more sophisticated method (called SSL for semi-supervised learning) to normalize local similarities is to map them to global similarities using a learned mapping function. A centralized sample document collection *CSD* is obtained by combining sampled documents from each search engine (Si and Callan, 2003a). *CSD* is treated as a representative of the global collection containing all documents in all search engines, and the similarities computed based on *CSD* and a global similarity function are considered as global similarities. Each query is sent to every selected component search engine to retrieve some documents and their local similarities. The global similarity of each retrieved document that appears in *CSD* is also computed. Then, based on several pairs of global and local similarities of some documents from each search engine, a mapping function can be derived based on regression.

Some of these merging algorithms further adjust the re-normalized local similarities by taking into account the estimated usefulness or quality of each search engine so as to give more preference to results retrieved from more useful search engines. The ranking score of the search engine computed in the search engine selection step reflects the usefulness of a search engine for a given query. Finally, the results retrieved from different search engines are ranked in descending order of their adjusted similarities by the result merger.

In CORI Net (Callan et al., 1995), the adjustment works as follows. Let *rs* be the ranking score of component search engine S and *av_rs* be the average of the ranking scores of all selected component search engines. Let *ls* be the local similarity of result r from D. Then the adjusted similarity of d is computed by $ls * (1 + N * (rs - av\_rs)/av\_rs)$, where N is the number of component search engines selected for the given query. Clearly, this adjustment increases (decreases) the local similarities of those results retrieved from search engines whose ranking scores are above (below) the average ranking score. In ProFusion (Gauch et al., 1996), the local similarity of each result is adjusted by simply multiplying it by the ranking score of the search engine that retrieved the result.

Most of today's search engines do not return similarities for retrieved results. As a result, the above local similarity normalization and adjustment techniques are no longer applicable for metasearch engines whose component search engines are autonomous and uncooperative. For the rest of this chapter, we will focus on result merging algorithms that do not use local similarities of retrieved results.

In general, for a result r retrieved by a component search engine S, the following information could be obtained and used for result merging:

- The full document of r: The full document can be downloaded using the URL of the Web page, which is usually included in the SRR of the result.
- The local rank of r: This is the rank position of r among the results returned by S for the given user query.
- The title of r: This is the title of the Web page for r, which is usually included in the SRR of the result.
- The URL of r: This is the URL of the Web page for r, which is usually included in the SRR of the result. Note that we can not only download the Web page using a URL, we can also often discover which organization/person published the Web page from the URL.
- The snippet of r: This is the short text excerpt from the Web page for r, which is usually included in the SRR of the result.
- The publication time of r: This is the time when the Web page for r was published. This information is often included in the SRR of the result when the result is time sensitive. For example, news search engines often include publication times of the retrieved news articles in the SRRs. If this information is provided in the SRR, the *last_modified* time of the Web page can be used instead.
- The size of r: This is the number of bytes of the Web page for r, which is usually included in the SRR of the result.
- The ranking score of S: This is the ranking score of S with respect to the user query and the score is computed by the search engine selector during the search engine selection step.

Not all of the above information has been used by existing result merging algorithms. In fact, most current result merging algorithms use a small subset of the above information.

In this chapter, we classify the result merging algorithms based on the types of information they use to perform the merging and present them based on this classification. For the rest of this chapter, we first present merging algorithms that use the full document of each retrieved result, then present several algorithms that primarily use the information that is available in the SRRs, and, finally, we present some algorithms that primarily use the local ranks of retrieved results.

5.1 MERGING BASED ON FULL DOCUMENT CONTENT

After a component search engine processes a user query sent from a metasearch engine, it returns a list of SRRs to the metasearch engine. In order to utilize the full document content of each result to perform result merging, the full documents of all these results need to be fetched from the Web sites that host them using the URLs in these SRRs.

Once the full documents have been fetched, the result merger can employ any global similarity function to compute their global similarities with the query. Consider the case in which the global similarity function is the *Cosine function*, and the global document frequency of each term is known to the metasearch engine (note that if the selected component search engines have no or little overlap, then the global document frequency of a term can be computed, approximately, as the sum of the document frequencies of the term in all selected search engines). After a document is downloaded, the term frequency of each term in the document can be obtained. As a result, all statistics (i.e., term frequency *tf* and document frequency *df* of each term) needed to compute the global similarity of the document will be available and the global similarity can be computed. After the global similarities of all retrieved documents are computed, the result merger ranks the results returned by different component search engines in descending order of their global similarities.

The result merging algorithm in the Inquirus metasearch engine (Lawrence and Lee Giles, 1998) computes the global similarity of each downloaded document d for a given query q using the following similarity function:

$$sim(d,q) = c_1 N_p + \left(c_2 - \frac{\sum_{i=1}^{N_p-1} \sum_{j=i+1}^{N_p} \min(d(i,j), c_2)}{\sum_{k=1}^{N_p-1} (N_p - k)} \right) \Big/ \left(\frac{c_2}{c_1} \right) + \frac{N_t}{c_3} \tag{5.1}$$

where N_p is the number of distinct query terms that appear in d, N_t is the total number of query term occurrences in d, $d(i, j)$ is the minimum distance (in terms of the number of characters) between the i-th and j-th of the query terms in d, c_1 is a constant that controls the overall magnitude of $sim(d, q)$, c_2 is a constant specifying the maximum distance between query terms, and c_3 is a constant specifying the importance of term frequency. In Inquirus, these settings are as follows: c_1 = 100, c_2 = 5000, and c_3 = $10*c_1$. If q has only one term, Inquirus simply uses the distance from the start of the document to the first occurrence of the term as an indicator of relevance. The above similarity function captures not only the terms in common between the query and the document but also the proximity of query terms in the document.

The result merging algorithm proposed by Rasolofo et al. (2003) first downloads the full documents of the results retrieved from all selected search engines to form a document collection, then represents each document as a vector of terms with weights, where the weights are computed based on *tf*idf*. Finally, a global similarity function is used to compute the global similarity of each document with the user query as if there is a text retrieval system for the formed document collection. The results are then ranked in descending order of the global similarities.

Algorithm OptDocRetrv is a full document based method that combines *document selection* (i.e., determining how many results to retrieve from each selected search engine (Meng et al., 2002)) and result merging (Yu et al., 1999). Suppose that m most similar documents across all search engines, with respect to a given query, are desired for some positive integer m. In Section 3.4.5, we introduced a method to rank search engines in descending order of the similarity of the most similar document in each search engine for a given query. Such a rank is an optimal rank for retrieving the m most similar documents. This rank can also be used to perform document selection and result merging as follows.

First, for some small positive integer k (e.g., k can start from 2), each of the k top ranked search engines is searched to obtain the actual global similarity of its most similar document. This may require downloading some documents from these search engines. Let min_*sim* be the minimum of these k similarities. Next, from these k search engines, all documents whose actual global similarities are greater than or equal to the tentative threshold min_*sim* are retrieved. If m or more documents have been retrieved, then this process stops. Otherwise, the next top ranked search engine (i.e., the $(k+1)$-th ranked search engine) will be considered, and its most similar document will be retrieved. The actual global similarity of this document is then compared with min_*sim*, and the minimum of these two similarities will be used as a new global threshold to retrieval all documents from these $k+1$ search engines whose actual global similarities are greater than or equal to this threshold. This process is repeated until m or more documents are retrieved. Finally, the retrieved documents are ranked in descending order of their actual global similarities. To reduce the possibility of invoking the same search engine multiple times during the above process, a larger number of results can be cached when a search engine is first invoked. Algorithm OptDocRetrv has the following property (Yu et al., 2002): If the search engines are optimally ranked and the m most similarity documents can be obtained from l search engines, then the algorithm invokes at most $l+1$ search engines to yield the m most similar documents.

Downloading documents and analyzing them on the fly can be an expensive undertaking, especially when the number of documents to be downloaded is large and the documents have large sizes. A number of remedies can be employed. First, downloading from different local systems can be carried out in parallel. Second, some documents can be analyzed first and displayed to the user so that further analysis can be done while the user reads the initial results (Lawrence and Lee Giles, 1998). The initially displayed results may not be correctly ranked, and the overall rank needs to be adjusted when more documents are analyzed. Third, we may consider downloading only the beginning portion of each (large) document for analysis (Craswell et al., 1999). As the bandwidth of the Internet improves, the delay caused by downloading documents on the fly should become less and less significant.

On the other hand, downloading-based approaches also have some clear advantages (Lawrence and Lee Giles, 1998). First, when trying to download documents, obsolete URLs can be identified. As a result, documents with dead URLs can be removed from the final result list. Second, by analyzing downloaded documents, documents will be ranked by their current contents. In contrast, local similarities may be computed based on old versions of these documents. Third, query terms in downloaded documents could be highlighted when displayed to the user without additional delay because these terms have already been identified when these documents were processed for computing their global similarities.

5.2 MERGING BASED ON SEARCH RESULT RECORDS

The search result records (SRRs) returned by most of today's search engines contain rich information about the retrieved results as described at the start of this chapter. In particular, the titles and snippets of the SRRs contain high quality content information that reflects the relevance of the corresponding documents with respect to the query topic. First, it is no secret that today's search engines give terms in the title of a page higher weights compared to terms in the body of the page. Second, the snippets are usually generated specifically for the submitted user query, and they are often the text fragment(s) in the documents that best match the query. Consequently, the title and snippet of a result can provide good clues as to whether the corresponding document is relevant to the query. Several result merging algorithms have been proposed to perform merging based on the information available in the retrieved SRRs, particularly the titles and snippets in the SRRs. We introduce some of these algorithms below.

The idea of utilizing titles and snippets of returned SRRs in result merging was first introduced by Tsikrika and Lalmas (2001) who proposed several methods[15]:

- **TSR Method**. TSR combines the title and snippet of each retrieved result into a single representative document. If a result is returned by multiple search engines, the representative will contain the title and all the snippets of the result. For each term in a representative, a weight is computed using only the term frequency information (document frequency information is not used because query terms will have high document frequencies among the retrieved results, which would negatively impact the importance of these terms if their *idf* weights were used). The similarity between a query and a representative is the sum of the weights of query terms in the representative. In the merged list, the results are ranked in descending order of the similarities of their representatives.

[15]We give a name to each method for easy reference.

- **TSRDS Method.** This method is a variation of TSR in that it models the result merging process using Dempster-Shafer's theory of evidence. The presence of a query term in a representative is treated as evidence about the result's relevance to the query, and the results are ranked in descending order of their combined evidence. A weight is assigned to the evidence of each term for each search engine based on the document frequency of the term among the representatives for the results from the search engine.

Rasolofo et al. (2003) propose a family of result merging algorithms using the information in SRRs. For a given piece of text T (i.e., title or snippet) from an SRR and a query q, the similarity between T and q, denoted as $sim(T, q)$, is defined as follows:

$$Sim(T, q) = \begin{cases} 100000 * |T \cap q| \Big/ \sqrt{|T|^2 + |q|^2}, & if \quad T \cap q \neq \Phi \\ 1000 - Rank, & if \quad T \cap q = \Phi \end{cases} \tag{5.2}$$

where $|X|$ is the length of X in number of terms and *Rank* is the local rank of the SRR. Only top 10 results from each component search engine are used to participate in the merging. In Formula (5.2), 1000 – *Rank* is used to give a non-zero similarity to the SRR even when T does not contain any query terms to reflect that the full document of the result must contain some query terms since it is ranked among the top 10 results. We now present the basic merging algorithms.

- **Algorithm TS** (Title Scoring). This algorithm computes the similarity between the user query and the title of each SRR using Formula (5.2) (i.e., T is the title) and ranks the results in descending order of these similarities.

- **Algorithm SS** (Snippet Scoring). This algorithm is the same as Algorithm TS except that title is replaced by snippet.

- **Algorithm TSS1** (Approach 1 for combining Title Scoring and Snippet Scoring). This algorithm works as follows. For each SRR, if its title contains at least one query term, then its similarity is computed by *Sim*(*Title*, q); else, if its snippet contains at least one query term, its similarity is computed by *Sim*(*Snippet*, q); and, finally, if neither the title nor the snippet contains a query term, its similarity is computed by 1000 – *Rank*. Then the results are ranked in descending order of these similarities. This algorithm gives preference to title over snippet based on the experiments showing that Algorithm TS has better performance than Algorithm SS.

- **Algorithm TSS2** (Approach 2 for combining Title Scoring and Snippet Scoring). In this algorithm, the similarity of an SRR is a weighted sum of its title score and its snippet score. A higher weight is given to the former (0.9) than to the latter (0.1).

Several variations to the above basic algorithms have also been introduced (Rasolofo et al., 2003). The first variation uses the publication date of each result to break ties in favor of more recently published results when multiple SRRs have the same similarities. The second variation computes a ranking score for each search engine and then uses these scores to adjust the similarities (only the $|T \cap Q| / \sqrt{|T|^2 + |Q|^2}$ part is adjusted). The adjustment increases the similarities for results returned from search engines having above average scores while reducing those from search engines having below average scores. The third variation estimates a precision-based usefulness score based on the search results of sample queries for each search engine, and then uses these scores to adjust the similarities in a similar manner as the above second variation.

A number of other SRR-based result merging algorithms have also been introduced (Lu et al., 2005).

- **Algorithm SRRSim.** This algorithm is similar to Algorithm TSS2 described above except the following three differences: (1) Different similarity functions are used for Algorithm SRRSim, specifically, the *Cosine similarity function* and the *Okapi function* are tested. (2) Equal weights are used to combine title-based similarity and the snippet-based similarity. (3) If the same document is retrieved from multiple search engines with different snippets (different search engines usually employ different ways to generate snippet), then the similarity between the query and each SRR will be computed, and the largest one will be used as the final similarity of this document for result merging.

- **Algorithm SRRRank.** This algorithm ranks SRRs using more features. The similarity function used in Algorithm SRRSim, whether it is the *Cosine function* or the *Okapi function*, may not be sufficiently powerful in reflecting the true matches of the SRRs with a given query. For example, these functions do not take proximity information such as how close the query terms occur in the title and snippet of an SRR into account, nor does it consider the order of appearances of the query terms in the title and snippet. Intuitively, if a query contains one or more phrases, then the order and proximity information can be significant to the match of phrases versus just individual terms.

  To better rank SRRs, the SRRRank algorithm considers five features related to the query terms: (1) The number of distinct query terms that appear in the title and the snippet (NDT). (2) The total number occurrences of the query terms that appear in the title and the snippet (TNT). (3) The locations of the occurred query terms (TLoc) in the SRR. (4) Whether the occurred query terms appear in the same order as they are in the query and whether they occur adjacently (ADJ). (5) The window size containing distinct occurred query terms (WS).

  Features 1 and 2 indicate the overlapping level between the query and the SRR. Usually, the larger the overlap is, the better their match is. There are three cases for feature 3: all in title, all in snippet, and scattered in both title and snippet. This feature describes the distribution of the query terms in the SRR. Title is usually given higher priority than the snippet. If all the occurred distinct query terms are located in the title or the snippet, the window size is the smallest number of consecutive words in the title or snippet that contains at least one occurrence of each occurred distinct query term; otherwise, the window size is considered to be infinite. Features 4 and 5 indicate how close the query terms appear in the SRR. Intuitively, the closer those terms appear in the SRR, the more likely they have the same meaning as they are in the query.

After the above pieces of information are collected for each SRR of the returned result, the SRRRank algorithm ranks the results as follows. First, the SRRs are divided into groups based on the number of distinct query terms (NDT) in their title and snippet fields. The groups having more distinct terms are ranked higher. Second, within each group, the SRRs are further divided into three sub-groups based on the location of the occurred distinct query terms (TLoc). The sub-group with these terms in the title ranks highest, followed by the sub-group with the distinct terms in the snippet, and the sub-group with the terms scattered in both title and snippet ranks last. Finally, within each sub-group, the SRRs that have more occurrences of query terms (TNT) that appear in the title and the snippet are ranked higher. If two SRRs have the same number of occurrences of query terms, first, the one with distinct query terms that appear in the same order and adjacently (ADJ) as they are in the query is ranked higher, and then, the one with smaller window size (WS) is ranked higher. After the above steps, if there is any tie, it is broken by the local ranks. The result with the higher local rank will have a higher global rank in the merged list. If a result is retrieved from multiple search engines, only the one with the highest global rank is kept.

- **Algorithm SRRSimMF**. This algorithm computes similarities between SRRs and the query using more features than the SRRSim algorithm. This algorithm is similar to SRRRank except that it quantifies the matches based on each feature identified in SRRRank so that the matching scores based on different features can be aggregated into a numeric value. Consider a given field of an SRR, say title (the same methods apply to snippet). For the number of distinct query terms in the title (NDT), its matching score is the ratio of NDT over the total number of distinct terms in the query (QLEN), denoted S_{NDT} = NDT / QLEN. For the total number of query terms in the title (TNT), its matching score is the ratio of TNT over the length of title TITLEN (i.e., the number of terms in the title), denoted S_{TNT} = TNT / TITLEN. For the query term order and adjacency information (ADJ), the matching score S_{ADJ} is set to 1 if the distinct query terms appear in the same order and adjacently in the title; otherwise, the value is 0. The window size (WS) of the distinct query terms in the processed title is converted into score S_{WS} = (TITLEN – WS) / TITLEN (smaller WS leads to larger score). All the matching scores of these features are aggregated into a single value, which is the similarity between the processed title T and q, using the following formula:

$$Sim(T,q) = S_{NDT} + \frac{1}{QLEN} * (w_1 * S_{ADJ} + w_2 * S_{WS} + w_3 * S_{TNT}) \tag{5.3}$$

where w_1, w_2 and w_3 are weight parameters.

For each SRR, the similarity between the title and the query ($Sim(T,q)$), and the similarity between the snippet S and the query ($Sim(S,q)$) are computed separately first and then merged into one value as follows:

$$Sim(SRR, q) = \frac{TNDT}{QLEN} * (c * Sim(T, q) + (1 - c) * Sim(S, q)) \quad (5.4)$$

where TNDT is the total number of distinct query terms that appear in the title and snippet. By multiplying by TNDT / QLEN, it is guaranteed that the SRR containing more distinct query terms will be ranked higher.

For metasearch engines whose component search engines have significant shared documents, the same result (based on the actual document, not the returned SRR), say R, may be retrieved from multiple component search engines. In this case, a method is needed to compute an overall similarity for R for the merging purpose. In Algorithm SRRSim described earlier, the maximum of the similarities between the query and all the SRRs that correspond to R is taken as the overall similarity for R for result merging.

The issue of combining the similarities for the same document that are computed by different retrieval systems has been well researched in the information retrieval community (see (Croft, W., 2000) for a good survey). One popular method is to perform a linear combination, i.e., a weighted sum of local similarities for the same document (Vogt and Cottrell, 1999). Several combination functions are also possible (Fox and Shaw, 1994; Lee, J., 1997). One combination function that performs well compared to other functions is *combMNZ*. For a given result R, this function can be expressed as *sumsim* * *nnzs*, where *sumsim* is the sum of the similarities of all the SRRs corresponding to R, and *nnzs* is the number of non-zero similarities for R, which is the same as the number of search engines that return R with non-zero similarities. For example, consider the case where there are four component systems and each system returns all results that have positive similarities. Suppose that, for result R, three of the four systems return a corresponding SRR. Then for this R, we have *nnzs* = 3. The good performance of *the combMNZ* function can be explained by the following observation about the results returned by different retrieval systems over the same document collection (Lee, J., 1997): Different retrieval systems tend to retrieve the same set of relevant documents but different sets of irrelevant documents.

The *combMNZ* function can be adopted to result merging for metasearch engines as follows: Use only those documents whose SRRs are ranked among the top K results, for some value K, by each component search engine for merging, i.e., if no SRR for a document is ranked among the top K results by a component search engine, this document is considered to have zero similarity by this search engine. Note that in practice, it is unrealistic to expect autonomous search engines to return all results that have non-zero similarity with a query.

5.3 MERGING BASED ON LOCAL RANKS OF RESULTS

In this section, we introduce several result merging algorithms that are primarily based on the local ranks of the retrieved results. These algorithms can be classified into the following four categories:

1. *Round-Robin based methods.* These methods take one result from the result list of each component search engine in each round in certain order.

2. *Similarity conversion based methods.* These methods convert the local ranks into similarities so that similarity-based merging techniques can be applied.

3. *Voting based methods.* These methods treat each component search engine as a voter and each result as a candidate in an election. Voting based techniques are more suitable for metasearch engines whose component search engines have substantial overlaps among their document collections.

4. *Machine learning based methods.* This type of method learns an overall rank for each result in the merged result list based on training data.

In the following discussion, we assume that N component search engines $\{S_1, \ldots, S_N\}$ are used to evaluate a given query q. Let $RL_i = (R_{i1}, R_{i2}, \ldots)$ be the list of results returned from S_i for q.

5.3.1 ROUND-ROBIN BASED METHODS

Several variations of round-robin based merging strategies exist (Rasolofo et al., 2003), which can be summarized into the following two algorithms.

- **Algorithm SimpleRR.** This simple round-robin method consists of two steps. In the first step, order the selected search engines arbitrarily. In the second step, take the results from the result lists of these search engines in a number of iterations or rounds, and sort the results in the same order the results are taken. In each round, take the next not-yet taken result from each RL_i, based on the search engine order obtained in Step 1. This process is repeated until all result lists are exhausted. If a result list is exhausted, the round-robin process continues with the remaining result lists. This simple merging method is unlikely to yield good performance because it considers all results with the same local rank to have the same likelihood to be relevant and ignores the fact that the usefulness of different selected search engines is usually different for a given query.

- **Algorithm PriorityRR.** This method improves Algorithm SimpleRR by giving priority to search engines that have higher ranking scores obtained during the search engine selection step. In other words, Algorithm PriorityRR differs from Algorithm SimpleRR only in the way the search engines are ordered, i.e., the former orders the search engines in descending order of their ranking scores while the latter uses a random ordering. Note that Algorithm PriorityRR does not take into consideration the differences between the search engine scores (i.e., only the order information is utilized).

The following is a randomized version of Algorithm PriorityRR (Voorhees et al., 1995). We will call this method Algorithm RandomRR.

- **Algorithm RandomRR**. Recall that the MRDD search engine selection method (see Section 3.2) first determines how many results to retrieve from each component search engine for a given query to maximize the precision of the retrieval. Suppose the desired number of results has been retrieved from each selected component search engine and the N result lists $RL_1, \ldots,$ RL_N have been obtained. To select the next result to be placed in the merged list, the rolling of a die is simulated. The die has N faces corresponding to the N result lists. Suppose n is the total number of results yet to be selected and n_i results are still in RL_i. The die is made biased such that the probability that the face corresponding to RL_i will be up when the die is rolled is n_i/n. When the face for RL_i is up, the current top ranked result in list RL_i is selected as the next highest ranked result in the merged list. After the selection, the selected result is removed from RL_i, and both n_i and n are reduced by 1. The probabilities are also updated accordingly. In this way, the retrieved results are ranked based on the probabilistic model.

5.3.2 SIMILARITY CONVERSION BASED METHODS

Methods for converting ranks to similarities have been proposed in several papers. Lee, J. (1997) uses the following function to convert a local rank to a similarity value:

$$Rank\_Sim(rank) = 1 - \frac{rank - 1}{num\_of\_retrieved\_docs} \tag{5.5}$$

This function assigns similarity 1 to the top ranked result; the similarities of other results depend on both the local ranks of the results and the total number of results that are retrieved. It can be seen that this function will assign a higher similarity to the same ranked result returned from a search engine that retrieved more results. For example, consider two search engines S_1 and S_2, and suppose for a given query, 10 results are retrieved from S_1 and 100 results are retrieved from S_2. Then based on Formula (5.5), the second ranked result from S_1 will have similarity 0.9 while the second ranked result from S_2 will have similarity 0.99. Based on this observation, a metasearch engine can improve the ranking of the results in the merged list that are returned from more useful search engines by retrieving more results from component search engines that have higher ranking scores, although this point was not considered by Lee, J. (1997).

In D-WISE (Yuwono and Lee, 1997), the following conversion method is used. For a given query q, let rs_i be the ranking score of search engine S_i, $rs_{\min}$ be the lowest ranking score among all search engines selected for q (i.e., $rs_{\min}$ = min{ rs_i }), and *rank* be the local rank of a result R from S_i. Recall that the ranking scores are numerical values, and the higher a score is, the better the corresponding search engine is for a given query. The following function converts *rank* to a similarity value:

$$sim(rank) = 1 - (rank - 1) * \frac{rs_{\min}}{m * rs_i} \tag{5.6}$$

where m is the number of results desired across all selected search engines. This conversion function has the following properties. First, all top-ranked results from component search engines will have the same converted similarity 1, just like Formula (5.5). This implies that all top-ranked results from component search engines are considered to be equally potentially useful. Second, the fraction in Formula (5.6), namely $F_i = rs_{\min}/(m * rs_i)$, is used to model the difference between the converted similarities of two consecutively ranked results from search engine S_i. In other words, the difference between the converted similarities of the j-th and the $(j+1)$-th ranked results from S_i is F_i. The difference is larger for search engines with smaller ranking scores. As a result, if the rank of result R from a search engine with a higher ranking score is the same as the rank of result R^* from a search engine with a lower ranking score but none of R and R^* is top-ranked, then the converted similarity of R will be larger than that of R^*. Consequently, this method tends to select more documents from search engines with higher-ranking scores into the merged result list.

Example 5.1 Consider two search engines S_1 and S_2. Suppose $rs_1 = 0.2$ and $rs_2 = 0.5$. Furthermore, suppose 4 results are desired from these two search engines. Then, we have $rs_{\min} = 0.2$, $F_1 = 0.25$ and $F_2 = 0.1$. Based on the conversion function (5.6), the top three ranked results from S_1 will have converted similarities $1, 0.75$, and 0.5, respectively, and the top three ranked results from S_2 will have converted similarities $1, 0.9$, and 0.8, respectively. As a result, the merged result list will contain three results from S_2 and one result from S_1. The results will be ranked in descending order of the converted similarities in the merged result list.

The SAFE (sample-agglomerate fitting estimate) method (Shokouhi and Zobel, 2009) converts local ranks to global similarities by utilizing the global similarities of some sampled documents from the same search engine. This method assumes that a centralized sample document collection *CSD* has been created in advance by sampling some documents from each component search engine. *CSD* can be created when sample documents are collected to generate the search engine representatives needed to support search engine selection (see Section 3.4.6). For component search engine S_i, let $SD(S_i)$ denote the set of sampled documents in *CSD* that are from S_i. For a given query q, the SAFE method consists of the following three steps:

1. Compute the global similarity between q and each document in $SD(S_i)$ using a global similarity function while treating the documents in $SD(S_i)$ as part of the document collection *CSD*. In other words, the collection statistics such as document frequencies for *CSD* are used to compute the weights of the terms for documents in $SD(S_i)$.

2. Determine where the documents in $SD(S_i)$ should be ranked among all the documents in S_i. There are two cases: (1) No documents in $SD(S_i)$ appear in the ranked result list RL_i returned by S_i for q, i.e., $SD(S_i) \cap RL_i = \Phi$. (2) $SD(S_i) \cap RL_i \neq \Phi$. In the former case, the returned documents in RL_i are assumed to be ranked ahead of all documents in $SD(S_i)$, and documents in $SD(S_i)$ are uniformly distributed among the ranks of all the documents in S_i with respect to q. Specifically, the k-th ranked result in $SD(S_i)$ based on its global similarity will be ranked at position $k^*|S_i|/|SD(S_i)|$ among all documents in S_i, where $|X|$ denotes the number of documents in X. In the latter case, the documents in $SD(S_i) \cap RL_i$ will be ranked as in RL_i and the remaining documents in $SD(S_i)$ will be ranked uniformly.

3. Estimate the global similarities of the documents in RL_i by curve fitting. Specifically, SAFE determines the relationship between the similarities of sampled documents and their estimated ranks by linear regression as in the following:

$$sim(d) = m * f(rank(d)) + e \tag{5.7}$$

where $sim(d)$ denotes the global similarity of a sampled document d in $SD(S_i)$ and $rank(d)$ is its estimated rank among the documents in S_i, m and e are two constants, and $f()$ is a function for mapping the document ranks into different distributions. Mapping functions that were tested for SAFE include $f(x) = x$, $f(x) = \ln x$, etc. For any given mapping function, based on the global similarities and ranks of the documents in $SD(S_i)$, the best fitting values for m and e can be estimated for search engine S_i. Then Formula (5.7) can be used to estimate the global similarities of other returned documents in RL_i based on their ranks. Finally, the results from all selected component search engines are ranked in descending order of the estimated global similarities in the merged result list.

5.3.3 VOTING BASED METHODS

As mentioned previously, in voting based methods, component search engines act as voters and retrieved results are treated as candidates in an election. In this election, we are not only interested in which candidate wins (i.e., ranked first in the merged result list) but also the ranking positions of all candidates. Ideally, each voter ranks all candidates and no tie is allowed. Translating this into the metasearch engine context, it means that each selected component search engine provides a ranked list of the same set of results. In practice, component search engines usually have different document collections, which implies that it is highly unlikely that, for any given query q, different result lists $RL_i = (R_{i1}, R_{i2}, \ldots)$ will contain the same set of results. Nevertheless, voting based methods are only suitable for metasearch engines whose component search engines have substantial overlaps among their document collections.

There are primarily two types of voting strategies. The first type includes different variations based on Borda's method, which is a positional method as it computes an overall score for each result based on its ranking positions in different local result lists and ranks the results in descending order of their overall score. The second type includes different variations based on Condorcet's method, which is a majoritarian method as it ranks a result higher (better) than another result in the merged result list only if the former is ranked higher than the latter in majority of the local result lists.

Borda's Methods

The following two Borda's methods are introduced for the metasearch context (Aslam and Montague, 2001).

- **Basic Borda-fuse.** This method assumes that the same set of results is retrieved by each selected component search engine. Suppose each result list RL_i contains n results. The basic Borda-fuse method assigns some points (score) to every result in its local result list to reflect the desirability of the result. It is required that every result receives some points and the total number of points used by each search engine is the same. A common point assignment strategy is as follows: The i-th ranked result in each list receives $(n - i + 1)$ points. Thus, the highest rank result in each list receives n points, followed by the next highest ranked result with $(n - 1)$ points, and so on. In practice, different result sets may be returned by different search engines. In this case, the union of the result sets from all selected search engines, denoted as URS, is used for point assignment. If URS has m results, then a total of $P_1 = 1 + 2 + \ldots + m$ points will be assigned to each list RL_i. The j-th ranked result in RL_i receives $(m - j + 1)$ points. If RL_i has k results, these results receive a total of $P_2 = \mathrm{m} + (m - 1) + \ldots + (m - k + 1)$ points. One way to use the remaining points, i.e., $(P_1 - P_2)$ points, is to distribute them equally to the results that are in URS but not in RL_i, which do not belong to RL_i but are now added to RL_i for merging purpose. For example, suppose for a user query, URS has 5 results $\{a, b, c, d, e\}$, which means the total number of points each search engine must assign is 1 + 2 + 3 + 4 + 5 = 15. If $RL_i = (a, c, e)$, then a, c, and e will be assigned 5, 4, and 3 points, respectively, and each of b and d will be assigned 1.5 points, which is half of the total points left, i.e., 3.

At the end of the point assignment process, each result in URS receives some points from each selected component search engine. The points for each result from all these search engines are then added. In the merged result list, results are ranked in descending order of their point sums.

- **Weighted Borda-fuse.** In this variation of Borda's method, each search engine is associated with a weight that reflects the overall quality or performance of the search engine. Let w_i be the weight of search engine S_i. A simple strategy for utilizing search engine weights is to multiply the points assigned to each result from S_i by w_i (Aslam and Montague, 2001). The weight associated with each search engine is its average precision based on a set of training queries. This weight is not sensitive to the specific user query in use. Using the ranking score of a search engine as its associated weight has been suggested (Meng and Yu., 2010). The advantage of this method is that the weight for each search engine is specifically related to the current query.

A method[16] that combines an SRR-based method (see Section 5.2) and a positional rank-based method is proposed by Tsikrika and Lalmas (2001). Let M1 be an SRR-based method (M1 is either Method TSR or Method TSRDS (Tsikrika and Lalmas, 2001), see Section 5.2). Let M2 be a rank-based method (the paper did not mention any specific method on assigning scores to rank positions, but Basic Borda-fuse could be such a method). Each of the two methods, namely M1 and M2, produces a list of ranked results. Method TSRR takes these two lists as input and applies M2 again to produce a final merged result list.

[16]We will call it Method TSRR for easy reference.

Condorcet's Methods

Given N local result lists, the basic idea of this class of methods is that the ranking of a result in the merged list should reflect the characteristics of all the result lists in the sense that if a result is ranked high in most of the result lists, then it should rank high in the merged list. Specifically, result R_i should be ranked higher than result R_j (i.e., R_i beats R_j) in the merged list if in majority of the N result lists, R_i is ranked higher than R_j. For example, consider three local result lists $RL_1 = (R_1, R_2, R_3)$, $RL_2 = (R_1, R_3, R_2)$, and $RL_3 = (R_2, R_1, R_3)$. It is easy to see that R_1 beats R_2, R_1 beats R_3 and R_2 beats R_3. Thus, a reasonable merged list is (R_1, R_2, R_3). In general, the relation *beat* is not transitive. For example, consider the following three local results: $RL_1 = (R_3, R_1, R_2)$, $RL_2 = (R_1, R_2, R_3)$, and $RL_3 = (R_2, R_3, R_1)$. In this case, we have R_1 beats R_2, R_2 beats R_3, but R_3 beats R_1. Given two results, R_i and R_j, if neither R_i beats R_j, nor R_j beats R_i, then we say that R_i and R_j are tied. Results in a cycle are also considered as ties (Montague and Aslam, 2002).

Condorcet's method and Borda's method often produce different merged results.

Example 5.2 Consider the two local result lists: $RL_1 = (R_1, R_2, R_3)$ and $RL_2 = (R_2, R_3, R_1)$. Based on Condorcet's method, R_1 and R_2 are tied because each beats the other exactly once, but based on Borda's method, R_2 will be ranked higher than R_1 in the merged list because R_2's total points are 5 while R_1's total points are 4. If we add another local result list $RL_3 = (R_1, R_2, R_3)$ to the above two lists, then based on Condorcet's method, R_1 will beat R_2, but based on Borda's method, R_1 and R_2 will be tied.

Some researchers have suggested that Condorcet's method has more desirable features than Borda's method as an election mechanism such as *anonymity* (equal treatment of all voters), *neutrality* (equal treatment of the candidates), and *monotonicity* (more support for a candidate does not jeopardize his/her election) (Montague and Aslam, 2002; Moulin, H., 1988). On the other hand, Borda's method is easier to implement than Condorcet's method.

The following Condorcet-fuse and Weighted Condorcet-fuse methods are proposed by Montague and Aslam (2002). Both methods assume that all local result lists contain the same set of results.

- **Condorcet-fuse**. Let RS be the set of results under consideration. This method sorts the results in RS based on the following comparison function between any two results R_i and R_j: if R_i is ranked higher than R_j in more than half of the local result lists, then rank R_i before R_j; otherwise, rank R_j before R_i. After the sorting is completed, this method outputs the sorted results as the merged result list.

This algorithm is shown to have the following properties (Montague and Aslam, 2002). First, it orders untied results correctly and tied results consecutively. Second, its complexity is $O(N * n \lg n)$, where N is the number of local result lists and n is the number of distinct results to be merged.

- **Weighted Condorcet-fuse**. This method first associates a weight to each component search engine. Then it replaces the comparison function in Condorcet-fuse by the following: If the sum of the weights of the search engines that rank R_i higher than R_j is larger than the sum of the weights of the search engines that rank R_j higher than R_i, then rank R_i before R_j (in the merged list); otherwise, rank R_j before R_i (in the merged list).

The discussions about search engine weight selection in the Weighted Borda-fuse method are applicable to the Weighted Condorcet-fuse method.

Several variations of the Condorcet's method have been proposed (Dwork et al., 2001). In the first method, an $n \times n$ matrix M is first constructed based on the N given result lists, where n is the number of distinct results in these result lists. The entries of the matrix are defined as follows. For $i \neq j$, $M[i, j] = 1$ if result R_j beats R_i, 0.5 if R_i and R_j are ties, and 0 if R_i beats R_j. $M[j, j] = n - (M[j, 1] + \ldots + M[j, j-1] + M[j, j+1] + \ldots + M[j, n])$. Intuitively, $M[j, j]$ is $n - n_j$, where n_j is the number of results that beat R_j, where a tie is counted as 0.5. Similarly, $M[1, j] + \ldots + M[j-1, j] + M[j+1, j] + \ldots + M[n, j]$ is the number of results that are beaten by R_j, denoted as m_j, again a tie is counted as 0.5. Thus, the sum of all entries in the j-th column is $C_j = n - n_j + m_j$. The result that beats all other results will have its column sum equals to $2n - 1$, while the result that is beaten by all other results will have its column sum equals to 1. Thus, one simple result merging algorithm is to rank the results in descending order of their column sums.

A variation of the above method is as follows. Compute $M'[i, j] = M[i, j]/n$ with the interpretation that there is a graph of n nodes (results), and $M'[i, j]$ is the transition probability for a surfer to move from result R_i to result R_j. If R_j beats R_i, the probability is positive; if R_j and R_i are ties, the probability is halved; and if R_i beats R_j, the probability is 0. The goal is to find the probabilities that the surfer will finally end up at the various nodes, similar to the way that PageRanks are computed (Page et al., 1998). Consider a random vector $V = [v_1, \ldots, v_n]$, where v_i is the probability that the surfer initially starts at R_i. Let $U_1 = V * M' = [u_1, \ldots, u_n]$, where u_i is the probability that R_i is reached after taking one transition as given by the matrix M'. If the transitions are repeated until $U_t = U_{t-1} * \mathrm{M}' = [u_1^*, \ldots, u_n^*]$, then u_i^* is the stationary probability that R_i is finally reached. This implies that U_k is the eigenvector of M' with eigenvalue 1. The results are then ranked in the merged list in descending order of their values in U_t.

Example 5.3 Consider the case where we have the following four local result lists: $RL_1 = (R_2, R_1, R_3)$, $RL_2 = (R_2, R_1, R_3)$, $RL_3 = (R_1, R_3, R_2)$, and $RL_4 = (R_3, R_2, R_1)$. Here, R_1 beats R_3, R_2 beats R_1, and R_2 ties R_3. The matrix M' is

$$\begin{bmatrix} 2/3 & 1/3 & 0 \\ 0 & 2.5/3 & 0.5/3 \\ 1/3 & 0.5/3 & 1.5/3 \end{bmatrix}.$$

U_t, the eigenvector of M' with eigenvalue $= 1$, is [0.2, 0.6, 0.2]. Therefore, one possible ranking of the three results is (R_2, R_1, R_3).

It is possible that U_t has a set of zero values and a set of positive values. Intuitively, the positive values correspond to *sinks* whereas the zero values correspond to sources such that if we start out from the sources, then eventually we end up in the sinks. The results corresponding to the positive values are ranked in non-ascending order according to their magnitudes and are ahead of the results with zero values. To rank the results corresponding to zero, the matrix M' is modified to eliminate the results that have been ranked. The remaining results are ranked by applying the same process on the modified M'. This process may be repeated until all results are ranked.

Example 5.4 Consider the following result lists: $RL_1 = (R_1, R_2, R_3)$, $RL_2 = (R_1, R_3, R_2)$, and $RL_3 = (R_2, R_1, R_3)$. For this example, R_1 beats R_2, R_1 beats R_3, and R_2 beats R_3. And the matrix M' is

$$\begin{bmatrix} 1 & 0 & 0 \\ 1/3 & 2/3 & 0 \\ 1/3 & 1/3 & 1/3 \end{bmatrix}.$$

Thus, U_t, the eigenvector of M' with eigenvalue $= 1$, is $[1, 0, 0]$. Therefore, R_1 is ranked first. After R_1 is eliminated and the modified matrix M' for the remaining results becomes

$$\begin{bmatrix} 1 & 0 \\ 1/2 & 1/2 \end{bmatrix}.$$

The new U_t is $[1, 0]$. Thus, R_2 is ranked second and R_3 is ranked third. The final ranking of the three results is (R_1, R_2, R_3).

5.3.4 MACHINE LEARNING BASED METHOD

Machine learning based result merging techniques require the use of training data to learn a merging model. The Bayes-fuse method (Aslam and Montague, 2001) is a learning-based method. This method is based on Bayesian inference. Let $r_i(R)$ be the local rank of result R returned by component search engine S_i (if R is not retrieved by S_i, $r_i(R) = \infty$ is assumed). This rank can be considered as the *evidence of relevance* for R provided to the result merger. Let $P_{rel} = \Pr(rel|r_1, \ldots, r_N)$ and $P_{irr} = \Pr(irr|r_1, \ldots, r_N)$ be the probabilities that R is *relevant* and *irrelevant*, given the ranks r_1, r_2, …, r_N, where N is the number of component search engines selected for the query. Based on the *optimal retrieval principle* in information retrieval, results with larger ratio $O_{rel} = P_{rel}/P_{irr}$ are more likely to be relevant.

Based on the Bayes rule, we have

$$P_{rel} = \frac{\Pr(r_1, \ldots, r_N|rel) * \Pr(rel)}{\Pr(r_1, \ldots, r_N)} \quad \text{and}$$

$$P_{irr} = \frac{\Pr(r_1, \ldots, r_N|irr) * \Pr(irr)}{\Pr(r_1, \ldots, r_N)}.$$

Thus,

$$O_{rel} = \frac{\Pr(r_1, \ldots, r_N|rel) * \Pr(rel)}{\Pr(r_1, \ldots, r_N|irr) * \Pr(irr)}.$$

By assuming that the local ranks assigned to relevant documents and irrelevant documents by different component search engines are independent, we have the following:

$$O_{rel} = \frac{\prod_{i=1}^{N} \Pr(r_i|rel) * \Pr(rel)}{\prod_{i=1}^{N} \Pr(r_i|irr) * \Pr(irr)} \quad \text{and}$$

$$\log O_{rel} = \sum_{i=1}^{N} \log \frac{\Pr(r_i|rel)}{\Pr(r_i|irr)} + \log \frac{\Pr(rel)}{\Pr(irr)}. \tag{5.8}$$

Note that rankings based on O_{rel} and $\log O_{rel}$ are the same. In addition, the second term in Formula (5.8) can be dropped without affecting the ranking because it is common to all results. Let $rel(R)$ denote the final value computed for result R, that is:

$$rel(R) = \sum_{i=1}^{N} \log \frac{\Pr(r_i(R)|rel)}{\Pr(r_i(R)|irr)}. \tag{5.9}$$

The Bayes-fuse method ranks results from all component search engines in descending order of $rel(R)$. The conditional probabilities in Formula (5.9) can be estimated from training data with known relevance judgment such as TREC data (Aslam and Montague, 2001).

CHAPTER 6

Summary and Future Research

This book provides a comprehensive coverage of the key technical issues related to the construction of metasearch engines that search text documents. Unlike most metasearch engines that have been developed in the past, which typically have a small number of component search engines, this book discusses metasearch engine technology from the angle of building large-scale metasearch engines that connect to thousands or more search engines. This book provides an in-depth analysis of the benefits that large-scale metasearch engines may bring and their advantages over regular metasearch engines and search engines. These benefits and advantages include increased search coverage of the Web, easier to reach the deep Web, likely better quality of contents, and potentially improved retrieval effectiveness. This book also discusses new technical challenges that need to be solved in order to build high quality large-scale metasearch engines. In general, highly scalable and automated solutions for several key components are needed.

This book describes an architecture of large-scale metasearch engines. Based on this architecture, a large-scale metasearch engine has three main components, namely, search engine selector, search engine incorporator and result merger. For each of these components, the technical challenges related to that component are analyzed and a number of representative solutions are reviewed. Often the solutions are divided into different categories based on a certain classification scheme. More specifically, for search engine selection, three learning-based methods, three sample documents based techniques, and five statistical representative approaches are reviewed. In addition, some methods for generating the representatives for statistical representative approaches are also described. For search engine incorporation, two sub-components, namely search engine connectors and search result extractors, are analyzed. For search engine connection, HTML search form and HTTP connection methods are reviewed. For search result extraction, three semiautomatic methods and four automatic methods are described. For result merging, three types of techniques based on what kinds of information are used to perform result merging are reviewed, including methods that use full document contents of retrieved results, methods that use primarily the returned search result records (SRRs), and methods that primarily use the local ranks of the retrieved results.

Much advancement in metasearch engine technology has been made in the last 15 years. A large number of commercial metasearch engines have been built and many are still operational on the Web although the exact number of active metasearch engines is unknown. A large-scale news metasearch engine, AllInOneNews (`http://www.allinonenew.com/`), having 1,800 component search engines, was launched by Webscalers in 2008, demonstrating that the current technology is already capable of building real large-scale metasearch engines.

Although much progress has been made in advanced metasearch engine technology, several significant technical challenges remain to be satisfactorily addressed, and these problems need to be solved before truly large-scale metasearch engine can be effectively built and managed. Below, we describe some of these challenges.

- **Search engine representative generation and maintenance**. Currently, the most effective search engine selection algorithms are those that employ statistics-based representatives. Although query-based sampling methods have been experimentally shown to generate search engine representatives of acceptable quality, they have not been shown to be practically viable for a large number of truly autonomous search engines. Certain statistics used by some search engine selection algorithms, such as the maximum normalized weight, is still too expensive to collect as it may require submitting a substantial number of queries to cover a significant portion of the vocabulary of a search engine. As the vocabularies of search engines can be very large and the number of search engines is also very large, the cost to generate good quality representatives can be prohibitively high. Furthermore, the important issue of how to effectively maintain the quality of representatives for search engines whose contents may change over time has started to get attention only recently (Ipeirotis et al., 2007), and more investigation into this issue is needed.

- **Automatic search engine connection with complex search forms**. Based on our observation, more search engines are employing more advanced tools to program their search forms. For example, more and more search forms now have Javascripts. Some search engines also include cookie and session id in their connection mechanism. These complexities make it significantly more difficult to automatically extract all needed connection information.

- **Automatic result wrapper generation for more complex format**. Current automatic wrapper generation techniques can achieve above 95% accuracy when the HTML response pages do not have Javascript, when the SRRs are displayed consecutively in a single column within a single section. However, accuracy goes down significantly when more complicated situations occur. For example, a method for extracting SRRs that are organized into different sections has an accuracy of about 80% on average (Zhao et al., 2006). More advanced techniques are needed to deal with these situations. We notice that among all current automatic wrapper generation methods, only ODE (Su et al., 2009) utilizes tag structures and visual features of response pages as well as domain ontologies in a single solution. However, only very limited visual features are used in ODE. In general, there is a lack of solutions that fully explore the capabilities of tag structures, visual features and domain ontologies at the same time.

- **Automatic maintenance**. Search engines used by metasearch engines may make various changes due to upgrade or other reasons. Possible changes may include search form change (e.g., add javascript), query format change (e.g., from Boolean to vector space query), and result display format change. These changes can cause the search engines not usable in the metasearch engines unless necessary adjustments are made automatically. Automatic metasearch engine maintenance is critical for the smooth operation of a large-scale metasearch engine, but this important problem remains largely unsolved. There are mainly two issues. One is to detect and differentiate various changes automatically, and the other is to fix the problem for each type of changes automatically.

- **More advanced result merging algorithm**. A large number of result merging algorithms have been proposed so far (see Chapter 5). However, most algorithms utilize only a small fraction of all available information for result merging. For example, rank-based solutions usually do not use the title and snippet information from SRRs. Intuitively, algorithms that effectively utilize the local ranks, titles, snippets and publication times of retrieved results, the ranking scores of component search engines, and the sample document collection consisting of sampled documents from each component search engine, are likely to perform better than solutions that utilize a small subset of the information.

- **Building a truly large-scale metasearch engine**. The number of specialized document-driven search engines on the Web is estimated to be over 20 million (Madhavan et al., 2007). A metasearch engine that can connect to a high percentage of these search engines, if built, will likely give Web users unprecedented search coverage of the Web. However, building a metasearch engine of such a scale involves many technical challenges beyond those we have discussed above. Some of these challenges include how to identify these search engines, how to measure the quality of these search engines (some of them may have very poor quality and should not be used), and how to identify and remove redundant search engines among them?

This book focuses on metasearch engines that search text documents. There is another type of metasearch engines that search structured data stored in backend database systems. This type of metasearch engines is sometimes called *database metasearch engines* or *Web database integration systems*. While some of the concepts and techniques introduced in this book, such as search engine connection and wrapper generation, are applicable to database metasearch engines, many new research and development issues arise from building this type of metasearch engine. These issues include how to extract and understand the search interface schemas of Web databases (such interfaces often have multiple search fields), how to integrate the search interfaces of multiple Web databases in the same domain into an integrated interface, and how to annotate the extracted data items (i.e., attribute values) with meaningful labels, etc. Some work related to these issues can be found at `http://www.cs.binghamton.edu/~meng/DMSE.html`[17].

[17] Accessed on November 3, 2010.

Bibliography

A. Arasu and H. Garcia-Molina. (2003) Extracting structured data from Web pages. In *Proc. ACM SIGMOD Int. Conf. on Management of Data*, pages 337–348, 2003. 73

J. Aslam and M. Montague. (2001) Models for metasearch. In *Proc. 24th Annual Int. ACM SIGIR Conf. on Research and Development in Information Retrieval*, pages 276–284, 2001. DOI: 10.1145/383952.384007 97, 98, 101, 102

R. A. Baeza-Yates and B. Ribeiro-Neto. (1999) *Modern Information Retrieval.* Addison-Wesley Longman Publishing Co., 1999. 6

R. Baumgartner, S. Flesca, and G. Gottlob. (2001) Visual Web information extraction with Lixto. In *Proc. 27th Int. Conf. on Very Large Data Bases*, pages 119–128, 2001a. 71

R. Baumgartner, S. Flesca, and G. Gottlob. (2001) Supervised wrapper generation with Lixto. In *Proc. 27th Int. Conf. on Very Large Data Bases*, pages 715–716, 2001b. 70, 71

A. Broder. (2002) A taxonomy of Web search. *ACM SIGIR Forum*, 36(2):3–10, 2002. DOI: 10.1145/792550.792552 5

D. Buttler, L. Liu, and C. Pu. (2001) A fully automated object extraction system for the World Wide Web. In *Proc. 21st Int. Conf. on Distributed Computing Systems*, paper 361, 2001. 73, 74, 75, 76

D. Cai, S. Yu, J. Wen, and W. Ma. (2003) Extracting content structure for Web pages based on visual representation. In *Proc. 5th Asian-Pacific Web Conference*, pages 406–417, 2003. 82

J. Callan, M. Connell, and A. Du. (1999) Automatic discovery of language models for text databases. In *Proc. ACM SIGMOD Int. Conf. on Management of Data*, pages 479–490, 1999. DOI: 10.1145/304181.304224 57, 58, 59

J. Callan, W. B. Croft, and S. Harding. (1992) The Inquery retrieval system. In *Proc. 3rd Int. Conf. Database and Expert Systems Appl.*, pages 78–83, 1992. 48

J. Callan, Z. Lu, and W. B. Croft. (1995) Searching distributed collections with inference networks. In *Proc. 18th Annual Int. ACM SIGIR Conf. on Research and Development in Information Retrieval*, pages 21–28, 1995. DOI: 10.1145/215206.215328 47, 85, 86

C. H. Chang, M. Kayed, M. R. Girgis, and K. F. Shaalan. (2006) A survey of Web information extraction systems. *IEEE Trans. Knowl. and Data Eng.*, 18(10):1411–1428, 2006. DOI: 10.1109/TKDE.2006.152 69, 70

comScore.com. (2010) *comScore Releases August 2010 U.S. Search Engine Rankings*. Available at `http://www.comscore.com/Press_Events/Press_Releases/2010/9/comScore_Releases_August_2010_U.S._Search_Engine_Rankings`. Accessed on October 18, 2010. 3

J. Cope, N. Craswell, and D. Hawking. (2003) Automated discovery of search interfaces on the Web. In *Proc. 14th Australasian Database Conf.*, pages 181–189, 2003. 65, 66

N. Craswell. (2000) *Methods in Distributed Information Retrieval*. Ph.D. thesis, School of Computer Science, The Australian National University, Canberra, Australia, 2000. 21

N. Craswell, D. Hawking, and P. Thistlewaite. (1999) Merging results from isolated search engines. In *Proc. 10th Australasian Database Conf.*, pages 189–200, 1999. 89

V. Crescenzi, G. Mecca, and P. Merialdo. (2001) RoadRunner: Towards automatic data extraction from large Web sites. In *Proc. 27th Int. Conf. on Very Large Data Bases*, pages 109–118, 2001. 73

W. B. Croft. (2000) Combining approaches to information retrieval. In W. B. Croft, editor, 2000 *Advances in Information Retrieval: Recent Research from the Center for Intelligent Information Retrieval*, pages 1–36, Kluwer Academic Publishers, 2000. 28, 93

W. B. Croft, D. Metzler, and T. Strohman. (2009) *Search Engines: Information Retrieval in Practice*. Addison-Wesley, 2009. 5, 8

M. Cutler, H. Deng, S. Manicaan, and W. Meng. (1999) A new study on using HTML structures to improve retrieval. In *Proc. 11th IEEE Int. Conf. on Tools with AI* pages 406–409, 1999. DOI: 10.1109/TAI.1999.809831 13, 14

Dogpile.com (2007) *Different Engines, Different Results*. 2007. Available at `http://www.infospaceinc.com/onlineprod/Overlap-DifferentEnginesDifferentResults.pdf`. Accessed on November 3, 2010. 26, 28

D. Dreilinger and A. Howe (1997) Experiences with selecting search engines using metasearch. *ACM Trans. on Information Syst.* 15(3):195–222, 1997. DOI: 10.1145/256163.256164 40, 85

C. Dwork, R. Kumar, M. Naor, and D. Sivakumar. (2001) Rank aggregation methods for the Web. In *Proc. 10th Int. World Wide Web Conf.*, pages 613–622, 2001. 100

D. W. Embley, Y. Jiang, and Y-K. Ng. (1999) Record-boundary discovery in Web-documents. In *Proc. ACM SIGMOD Int. Conf. on Management of Data*, pages 467–478, 1999. DOI: 10.1145/304181.304223 74, 76

Y. Fan and S. Gauch. (1999) Adaptive agents for information gathering from multiple, distributed information sources. In *Proc. AAAI Symp. on Intelligent Agents in Cyberspace*, pages 40–46, 1999. DOI: 10.1145/371920.372165 41

E. A. Fox and J. A. Shaw. (1994) Combination of multiple searches In *Proc. The 2nd Text Retrieval Conf.*, pages 243–252, 1994. 93

W. Frakes and R. Baeza-Yates. (1992) *Information Retrieval: Data Structures and Algorithms*. Prentice-Hall, 1992. 5

S. Gauch, G. Wang, and M. Gomez. (1996) Profusion: Intelligent fusion from multiple, distributed search engines. *Journal of Universal Computer Science* 2(9):637–649, 1996. DOI: 10.3217/jucs-002-09-0637 41, 85, 86

L. Gravano, C-C. K. Chang, and H. Garcia-Molina. (1997) STARTS: Stanford proposal for internet meta-searching. In *Proc. ACM SIGMOD Int. Conf. on Management of Data*, pages 207–218, 1997. DOI: 10.1145/253260.253299 34, 57

L. Gravano and H. Garcia-Molina. (1995) Generalizing gloss to vector-space databases and broker hierarchies. International In *Proc. 21th Int. Conf. on Very Large Data Bases*, pages 78–89, 1995. 49

T. Haveliwala. (1999) Efficient computation of PageRank. *Technical Report*. Department of Computer Science, Stanford University, Stanford, California, 1999. 16, 17

D. Hiemstra. (2008) Amit Singhal revealed exact formula of Google's ranking at Retrieval Conference in Glasgow. Available at `http://www.sigir.org/sigir2007/news/20080401singhal.html`, 2008. Accessed November 3, 2010. 32

A. Hogue and D. Karger. (2005) Thresher: Automating the unwrapping of semantic content from the World Wide Web. In *Proc. 14th Int. World Wide Web Conf.*, pages 86–95, 2005. DOI: 10.1145/1060745.1060762 70, 72

C. Hsu and M. Dung. (1998) Generating finite-state transducers for semistructured data extraction from the Web. *Information Systems*, 23(8):521–538, 1998. DOI: 10.1016/S0306-4379(98)00027-1 70

P. G. Ipeirotis and L. Gravano. (2002) Distributed search over the hidden Web: hierarchical database sampling and selection. In *Proc. 28th Int. Conf. on Very Large Data Bases*, pages 394–405, 2002. DOI: 10.1016/B978-155860869-6/50042-1 58, 59

P. G. Ipeirotis, A. Ntoulas, J. Cho, and L. Gravano. (2007) Modeling and managing changes in text databases. *ACM Trans. Database Syst.* 32(3), article 14, 2007. DOI: 10.1145/1272743.1272744 104

B. Kahle and A. Medlar. (1991) An information system for corporate users: wide area information servers. *ConneXions – The Interoperability Report*, 5(11):2–9, 1991. 39

M. Koster. (1994) Aliweb: Archie-like indexing in the Web. *Computer Networks and ISDN Systems* 27(2):175–182, 1994. DOI: 10.1016/0169-7552(94)90131-7 38

N. Kushmerick. (1997) *Wrapper Induction for Information Extraction* Ph.D. thesis, Department of Computer Science and Engineering, University of Washington, Seattle, Washington, 1997. 70

N. Kushmerick, D. Weld, and R. Doorenbos. (1997) Wrapper induction for information extraction. In *Proc. 15th Int. Joint Conf. on AI*, pages 729–735, 1997. 70

A. Laender, B. Ribeiro-Neto, A. da Silva, and J. Teixeira. (2002) A brief survey of Web data extraction tools. *ACM SIGMOD Rec.*, 31(2):84–93, 2002. DOI: 10.1145/565117.565137 69

S. Lawrence and C. Lee Giles. (1998) Inquirus, the NECI meta search engine. In *Proc. 7th Int. World Wide Web Conf.,* pages 95–105, 1998. DOI: 10.1016/S0169-7552(98)00095-6 87, 88, 89

J. Lee. (1997). 1997 Analyses of multiple evidence combination. In *Proc. 20th Annual Int. ACM SIGIR Conf. on Research and Development in Information Retrieval*, pages 267–276, 1997. DOI: 10.1145/258525.258587 28, 93, 95

K. Liu, W. Meng, J. Qiu, C. Yu, V. Raghavan, Z. Wu, Y. Lu, H. He, and H. Zhao. (2007) AllInOneNews: Development and evaluation of a large-scale news metasearch engine. In *Proc. ACM SIGMOD Int. Conf. on Management of Data*, Industrial track, pages 1017–1028, 2007. DOI: 10.1145/1247480.1247601 56, 80

K. Liu, C. Yu, and W. Meng. (2002) Discovering the representative of a search engine. In *Proc. Int. Conf. on Information and Knowledge Management*, pages 652–654, 2002a. DOI: 10.1145/584792.584909 52

K. Liu, C. Yu, W. Meng, W. Wu, and N. Rishe. (2002) A statistical method for estimating the usefulness of text databases. *IEEE Trans. Knowl. and Data Eng.*, 14(6):1422–1437, 2002b. DOI: 10.1109/TKDE.2002.1047777 59

W. Liu, X. Meng, and W. Meng. (2010) ViDE: A vision-based approach for deep Web data extraction. *IEEE Trans. Knowl. and Data Eng.*, 22(3):447–460, 2010. DOI: 10.1109/TKDE.2009.109 74, 82

Y. Lu, W. Meng, L. Shu, C. Yu, and K. Liu. (2005) Evaluation of result merging strategies for metasearch engines. In *Proc. 6th Int. Conf. on Web Information Systems Eng.*, pages 53–66, 2005. DOI: 10.1007/11581062_5 91

J. Madhavan, S. Cohen, X. Dong, A. Halevy, A. Jeffery, D. Ko, and C. Yu. (2007) Web-scale data integration: You can afford to pay as you go. In *Proc. 3rd Biennial Conf. on Innovative Data Systems Research*, pages 342–350, 2007. 105

J. Madhavan, D. Ko, L. Kot, V. Ganapathy, A. Rasmussen, and A. Y. Halevy. (2008) Google's deep Web crawl. In *Proc. 34th Int. Conf. on Very Large Data Bases*, pages 1241–1252, 2008. DOI: 10.1145/1454159.1454163 27

U. Manber and P. Bigot. (1997) The Search broker. In *Proc. 1st USENIX Symp. on Internet Tech. and Systems*, pages 231–239, 1997. 39

U. Manber and P. Bigot. (1998) Connecting diverse Web search facilities. *Data Engineering Bulletin*, 21(2):21–27, 1998. 39

B. B. Mandelbrot. (1988) *Fractal Geometry of Nature*. W. H. Freeman & Co, 1988. 59

C. D. Manning, P. Raghavan, and H. Schultze. (2008) *Introduction to Information Retrieval*. Cambridge University Press, 2008. 5

W. Meng, K. Liu, C. Yu, X. Wang, Y. Chang, and N. Rishe. (1998) Determine text databases to search in the internet. In *Proc. 24th Int. Conf. on Very Large Data Bases*, pages 14–25, 1998. 52

W. Meng, K. Liu, C. Yu, W. Wu, and N. Rishe. (1999) Estimating the usefulness of search engines. In *Proc. 15th Int. Conf. on Data Engineering*, 146–153, 1999a. DOI: 10.1109/ICDE.1999.754917 53

W. Meng, Z. Wu, C. Yu, and Z. Li. (2001) A highly-scalable and effective method for metasearch. *ACM Trans. Information Syst.*, 19(3):310–335, 2001. DOI: 10.1145/502115.502120 56

W. Meng and C. Yu. (2010) Web Search Technologies for Text Documents. In H. Bidgoli, editor, *The Handbook of Technology Management*, Volume 3, article 31, Wiley Publishers, 2010. 98

W. Meng, C. Yu, and K. Liu. (1999) Detection of heterogeneities in a multiple text database environment. In *Proc. Int. Conf. on Cooperative Information Systems*, pages 22–33, 1999b. DOI: 10.1109/COOPIS.1999.792150 31, 53

W. Meng, C. Yu, and K. Liu. (2002) Building efficient and effective metasearch engines. *ACM Comput. Surv.*, 34(1):48–89, 2002. DOI: 10.1145/505282.505284 31, 37, 39, 88

R. Motwani and P. Raghavan. (1995) *Randomized Algorithms*. Cambridge University Press, 1995. 16

M. H. Montague and J. A. Aslam. (2002) Condorcet fusion for improved retrieval. In *Proc. Int. Conf. on Information and Knowledge Management*, pages 538–548, 2002. DOI: 10.1145/584792.584881 99

H. Moulin. (1988) *Axioms of Cooperative Decision Making*. Cambridge University Press, 1988. 99

I. Muslea, S. Minton, and C. A. Knoblock. (1999) A hierarchical approach to wrapper induction. In *Proc. Int. Conf. on Autonomous Agents*, pages 190–197, 1999. DOI: 10.1145/301136.301191 70

Standards Committee BC / Task Group 3. (2006) *NISO Metasearch Initiative: Metasearch XML Gateway Implementers Guide (Version 1.0)*. NISO Press, 2006. Available at `http://www.niso.org/publications/rp/RP-2006--02.pdf`. Accessed on November 3, 2010. 35

National Information Standards Organization. (2006a) *Collection Description Specification*. NISO Press, 2006a. Available at `http://www.niso.org/workrooms/mi/Z39--91-DSFTU.pdf`. Accessed on November 3, 2010. 35, 36

National Information Standards Organization. (2006b) *Information Retrieval Service Description Specification*. NISO Press, 2006b. Available at `http://www.niso.org/workrooms/mi/Z39--92-DSFTU.pdf`. Accessed on November 3, 2010. 35

L. Page, S. Brin, R. Motwani, and T. Winograd. (1998) The PageRank citation ranking: Bring order to the Web. Technical Report, Department of Computer Science, Stanford University, Stanford, California, 1998. 14, 16, 100

J. M. Ponte and W. B. Croft. (1998) A language modeling approach to information retrieval. In *Proc. 21st Annual Int. ACM SIGIR Conf. on Research and Development in Information Retrieval*, pages 275–281, 1998. DOI: 10.1145/290941.291008 8

D. Quan, D. Huynh, and D. R. Karger. (2003) Haystack: A platform for authoring end user semantic Web applications. In *Proc. 2nd Int. Semantic Web Conf.*, pages 738–753, 2003. DOI: 10.1007/978-3-540-39718-2_47 72

S. Raghavan and H. Garcia-Molina. (2001) Crawling the hidden Web. In *Proc. 27th Int. Conf. on Very Large Data Bases*, pages 129–138, 2001. 27

Y. Rasolofo, D. Hawking, and J. Savoy. (2003) Result merging strategies for a current news metasearcher. *Information Proc. & Man.*, 39(4):581–609, 2003. DOI: 10.1016/S0306-4573(02)00122-X 88, 90, 94

S. E. Robertson and K. Sparck Jones. (1976) Relevance weighting of search terms. *J. American. Soc. for Information Sci. & Tech.*, 27:129–146, 1976. DOI: 10.1002/asi.4630270302 8

S. E. Robertson and S. Walker. (1999) Okapi/Keenbow at TREC-8. In *Proc. The 8th Text Retrieval Conf.*, pages 151–161, 1999. 8

G. Salton and M. J. McGill. (1983) *Introduction to Modern Information Retrieval*. McGraw-Hill, 1983. 5, 7

G. Salton. (1989) *Automatic Text Processing: The Transformation, Analysis, and Retrieval of Information by Computer*. Addison Wesley, 1989. 32

E. Selberg and O. Etzioni. (1997) The metacrawler architecture for resource aggregation on the Web. *IEEE Expert*, 12(1):8–14, 1997. DOI: 10.1109/64.577468 85

M. Shokouhi. (2007) Central-rank-based collection selection in uncooperative distributed information retrieval. In *Proc. 29th European Conf. on IR Research*, pages 160–172, 2007. DOI: 10.1007/978-3-540-71496-5_17 45, 46

M. Shokouhi and J. Zobel. (2009) Robust result merging using sample-based score estimates. *ACM Trans. Information Syst.*, 27(3):1–29, 2009. DOI: 10.1145/1508850.1508852 96

M. Shokouhi and L. Si. Federated Search. *Foundations and Trends in Information Retrieval*, 2011 (in press). 21, 43, 59

L. Si and J. Callan. (2003) A semisupervised learning method to merge search engine results. *ACM Trans. Information Syst.*, 21(4):457–491, 2003a. DOI: 10.1145/944012.944017 85

L. Si and J. Callan. (2003) Relevant document distribution estimation method for resource selection. In *Proc. 26th Annual Int. ACM SIGIR Conf. on Research and Development in Information Retrieval*, pages 298–305, 2003b. DOI: 10.1145/860435.860490 43, 44

L. Si and J. Callan. (2004) Unified utility maximization framework for resource selection. In *Proc. Int. Conf. on Information and Knowledge Management*, pages 32–41, 2004. DOI: 10.1145/1031171.1031180 44

C. Silverstein, M. Henzinger, H. Marais, and M. Moriciz. (1999) Analysis of a very large Web search engine query log. *ACM SIGIR Forum*, 33:6–12, 1999. DOI: 10.1145/331403.331405 4

K. Simon and G. Lausen. (2005) ViPER: Augmenting automatic information extraction with visual perceptions. In *Proc. Int. Conf. on Information and Knowledge Management*, pages 381–388, 2005. DOI: 10.1145/1099554.1099672 74

W. Su, J. Wang, and F. H. Lochovsky. (2009) ODE: Ontology-assisted data extraction. *ACM Trans. Database Syst.*, 34(2), article 12, 2009. DOI: 10.1145/1538909.1538914 74, 80, 104

A. Sugiura and O. Etzioni. (2000) Query routing for Web search engines: Architecture and experiments. In *Proc. 9th Int. World Wide Web Conf.*, pages 417–429, 2000. DOI: 10.1016/S1389-1286(00)00059-1 39

K-C. Tai. (1979) The tree-to-tree correction problem. *J. ACM*, 26(3):422–433, 1979. DOI: 10.1145/322139.322143 72

T. Tsikrika and M. Lalmas. (2001) Merging techniques for performing data fusion on the Web. In *Proc. Int. Conf. on Information and Knowledge Management*, pages 127–134, 2001. DOI: 10.1145/502585.502608 89, 98

H. Turtle and W. B. Croft. (1991) Evaluation of an inference network-based retrieval model. *ACM Trans. Information Syst.*, 9(3):8–14, 1991. DOI: 10.1145/125187.125188 48

H. Turtle and J. Flood. (1995) Query evaluation: Strategies and optimizations. *Information Proc. & Man*, 31:831–850, 1995. DOI: 10.1016/0306-4573(95)00020-H 9, 10

B. Ussery. (2008) Google – average number of words per query have increased! 2008. Available at `http://www.beussery.com/blog/index.php/2008/02/google-average-number-of-words-per-query-have-increased/`. Accessed on November 3, 2010. 4

C. C. Vogt and G. W. Cottrell. (1999) Fusion via a linear combination of scores. *Information Retrieval*, 1(3):151–173, 1999. DOI: 10.1023/A:1009980820262 93

E. M. Voorhees, N. Gupta, and B. Johnson-Laird. (1995) Learning collection fusion strategies. In *Proc. 18th Annual Int. ACM SIGIR Conf. on Research and Development in Information Retrieval*, pages 172–179, 1995. DOI: 10.1145/215206.215357 40, 94

E. M. Voorhees and D. K. Harman. (2005) *TREC: Experiment and Evaluation in Information Retrieval*. The MIT Press, 2005. 11

J. Wang and F. H. Lochovsky. (2003) Data extraction and label assignment for Web databases. In *Proc. 12th Int. World Wide Web Conf.*, pages 187–196, 2003. DOI: 10.1145/775152.775179 73, 81

Y. Wang and D. DeWitt. (2004) Computing PageRank in a distributed internet search engine system. In *Proc. 30th Int. Conf. on Very Large Data Bases*, pages 420–431, 2004. 30

Z. Wu, W. Meng, C. Yu, and Z. Li. (2001) Towards a highly-scalable and effective metasearch engine. In *Proc. 10th Int. World Wide Web Conf.*, pages 386–395, 2001. DOI: 10.1145/371920.372093 55

Z. Wu, V. Raghavan, H. Qian, V. Rama K, W. Meng, H. He, and C. Yu. (2003) Towards automatic incorporation of search engines into a large-scale metasearch engine. In *Proc. IEEE/WIC Int. Conf. Web Intelligence*, pages 658–661, 2003. DOI: 10.1109/WI.2003.1241290 65

J. Xu and J. Callan. (1998) Effective retrieval with distributed collections. In *Proc. 21st Annual Int. ACM SIGIR Conf. on Research and Development in Information Retrieval*, pages 112–120, 1998. DOI: 10.1145/290941.290974 49

J. Xu and W. B. Croft. (1996) Query expansion using local and global document analysis. In *Proc. 19th Annual Int. ACM SIGIR Conf. on Research and Development in Information Retrieval*, pages 4–11, 1996. DOI: 10.1145/243199.243202 49

Y. Yang and H. Zhang. (2001) HTML page analysis based on visual cues. In *Proc. 6th Int. Conf. Document Analysis and Recognition*, pages 859–864, 2001. DOI: 10.1109/ICDAR.2001.953909 74

C. Yu, K. Liu, W. Meng, Z. Wu, and N. Rishe. (2002) A methodology to retrieve text documents from multiple databases. *IEEE Trans. Knowl. and Data Eng.*, 14(6):1347–1361, 2002. DOI: 10.1109/TKDE.2002.1047772 54, 88

C. Yu, W. Meng, K. Liu, W. Wu, and N. Rishe. (1999) Efficient and effective metasearch for a large number of text databases. In *Proc. Int. Conf. on Information and Knowledge Management*, pages 217–224, 1999. DOI: 10.1145/319950.320005 88

C. Yu and G. Salton. (1976) Precision weighting – an effective automatic indexing method. *J. ACM*, 23:76–88, 1976. DOI: 10.1145/321921.321930 8

B. Yuwono and D. Lee. (1997) Server ranking for distributed text resource systems on the internet. In *Proc. 5th Int. Conf. on Database Systems for Advanced Applications*, pages 391–400, 1997. 46, 95

C. Zhai and J. Lafferty. (2004) A study of smoothing methods for language models applied to information retrieval. ACM *Trans. Information Syst.*, 22:179–214, 2004. DOI: 10.1145/984321.984322 8

Y. Zhai and B. Liu. (2006) Structured data extraction from the Web based on partial tree alignment. *IEEE Trans. Knowl. and Data Eng.*, 18(12):1614–1628, 2006. DOI: 10.1109/TKDE.2006.197 74, 82

H. Zhao, W. Meng, Z. Wu, V. Raghavan, and C. Yu. (2005) Fully automatic wrapper generation for search engines. In *Proc. 14th Int. World Wide Web Conf.*, pages 66–75, 2005. DOI: 10.1145/1060745.1060760 74, 76, 78, 79

H. Zhao, W. Meng, and C. Yu. (2006) Automatic extraction of dynamic record sections from search engine result pages. In *Proc. 32nd Int. Conf. on Very Large Data Bases*, pages 989–1000, 2006. 104

P. M. Zillman. (2009) *Deep Web Research 2010*. 2009. Available at `http://www.llrx.com/features/deepweb2010.htm`. Accessed on November 3, 2010. 1

Authors' Biographies

WEIYI MENG

Weiyi Meng is currently a professor in the Department of Computer Science of the State University of New York at Binghamton. He received his Ph.D. in Computer Science from University of Illinois at Chicago in 1992. At the same year, he joined his current department as a faculty member. He is a co-author of the book *Principles of Database Query Processing for Advanced Applications*. He has published over 100 papers. He has served as general chair and program chair of several international conferences and as program committee members of over 50 international conferences. He is on the editorial board of the World Wide Web Journal and a member of the Steering Committee of the WAIM conference series. In recent years, his research has focused on metasearch engine, Web data integration, Internet-based information retrieval, information extraction and sentiment analysis. He has done pioneering work in large-scale metasearch engines. He is a co-founder of an Internet company (Webscalers) and serves as its president. His company has developed the world's largest news metasearch engine AllInOneNews.

CLEMENT T. YU

Clement T. Yu is a professor of computer science at the University of Illinois at Chicago. His research interests include multimedia information retrieval, metasearch engine, database management, and applications to healthcare. He has published more than 200 papers in these areas, and he is a co-author of the book *Principles of Database Query Processing for Advanced Applications*. Dr. Yu served as chairman of the ACM SIGIR and has extensive experience as a consultant in the fields of query processing in distributed and heterogeneous environments, including document retrieval. He was an advisory committee member for the National Science Foundation and was on the editorial boards of IEEE Transactions on Knowledge and Data Engineering, the Journal of Distributed and Parallel Databases, the International Journal of Software Engineering and Knowledge Engineering, and WWW: Internet and Web Information Systems. He also served as the General Chair of the ACM SIGMOD Conference and Program Committee Chair of the ACM SIGIR Conference. He is a co-founder of two Internet companies, Webscalers and PharmIR.

Printed in the United States
by Baker & Taylor Publisher Services